A WHISTLING WOMAN IS UP TO NO GOOD

Finding Your Wild Woman

LAUREL KING

CELESTIALARTS
Berkeley, California

Cover Illustration by Lauren Veen
Cover and text design by David Charlsen
Composition by ImageComp

FIRST CELESTIAL ARTS PRINTING 1993

Library of Congress Cataloging-in-Publication Data

King, Laurel.
    A whistling woman is up to no good : finding your wild woman / Laurel King.
        p.   cm.
    ISBN 0-89087-696-7 : $12.95
    1. Women—Psychology. 2. Self-actualization (Psychology) 3. Wild women. I. Title.
HQ1206.K467 1993
155.6'33—dc20   93-7867
                                                                CIP

4 5 6 7 8 / 99 98 97 96 95

Dedicated to
Chris Berger

TABLE OF CONTENTS

Acknowledgments

I want to acknowledge my husband, Chris Berger, for supporting me in a million ways. Your love and faith for me astounds
me, not to mention the dinners and care of Lily. Thank you Lily,
walking miracle, child of love. I know it hurt when I was away,
but you and your Papa are always in my heart.

Thank you my wonderful stepson Christopher Berger.
You are a wild inspiration.

I thank my friend, Alison Keye, for editing several chap-
ters, but most of all for encouraging me to let my wild woman
out. Thank you Jill Kelly, Susan King, Constance Savage, and
Susan Wright for your feedback and encouragement.

David Charlsen, you *are* an Honorary Whistling Woman.
Besides being the finest of editors, you created a cover that an
author can only dream will one day be hers. It was a gift from
your soul. You are a true Renaissance man.

Peter Beren, my agent, suggested I write this book years
ago. I finally got around to it. Thank you Peter. I'm not sure I
would have done it without your nudging.

Susan Wright, thank you for your outstanding computer
expertise, continuous support and the 1:30 a.m. mornings when
we couldn't even remember each other's names.

My friends, thank you for living with me through this
journey. Thank you Nancy Terry, Joni McConnell, Leslie Lindig,
Jill Kelly, Susan King, Constance Bennett, Jim Chambers and
Anne DeChenne for listening to my endless adventures, and
for feeding and housing me when necessary. And to all my
other Whistling friends: Mary Beth McClure, Lauren Hamilton,
John Moritz, Rhonda Zeilenga, Susan and Don McNeil, Sherry
Hilaski, Jackie Dornan, musicman Gerard Eisenberg, Lu Ross,
Maureen Montclair, Janice Winfrey, Kathleen Holland, Cathryn
Taylor, Berjé Baruch, Marvin Baker, Caryn Reardon, Betsy Baker,
Trish O'Connor, Junardi Armstrong, Marty Raphael, Anna
Franklin, Scott Swann, Ed O'Connell, John Maloney, Dee Shan-
non, Glenda Queen, Laura Davis, and Greg River.

Thank you miracle godmother, Cathryn Taylor, for the consistent love and devotion you have given Lily. Also, for what we have learned about grief from one another.

I want to acknowledge my parents, Lucille and Jim Dolan, for supporting my creativity, as a child, and for marketing my books with such passion.

Thank you to all the beautiful women who shared their stories for us to read. Thank you to the wild women who are in the documentary *A Whistling Woman Is Up to No Good* — what a gift. And I'd like to thank the crew, all of who will be listed in the credits of the movie.

I thank my brilliant therapist, Linda Eberth, who has seen me through it all. Thank you for the information Dr. Richard Gibb and Dr. Philip Kavanaugh willingly provided.

Thank you to Susan and Don McNeil, Kathy and Neil Munderloh, Caryn Reardon, Marc Pritchard, and Byron and Suzanne Kepford for letting me borrow their peaceful studios.

For child care, besides Chris and Cathryn Taylor, I want to thank Gerard Eisenberg, Sherry Hilaski, Katharine White and Lucille Dolan, and the best of child-care workers, Holly Guggenheim and Betsy Mulholland.

Thank you Publisher David Hinds, Managing Editor Veronica Randall and the staff of Celestial Arts Publishing for believing in *A Whistling Woman Is Up To No Good*.

Most of all, I am grateful to my Higher Power for being with me on this amazing journey through life.

1

The Wild Woman

Introduction

A wild woman is extraordinarily herself. She does what is natural to her without inhibitions, which means she can do and be anything. A wild woman is spontaneous, bold, sexually alive and takes risks, leaps before she thinks and is willing to express all of herself. She is untamed by herself or others. She says and does what she feels. She can be quiet and thoughtful, fierce and angry. She's joyful, laughs loudly, plays hard, screams and mourns her losses. A wild woman will at times be unsettling to herself and others. She can even be (oh, no!) offensive. She is loved by many, but can be threatening to others. She has discovered her wild nature and is willing to express it.

That wild nature is in us all. Isadora Duncan, Madonna and Josephine Baker are famous for their flamboyance, yet that kind of exuberance may not be your style. The way you choose to express your wild side will depend on your individual nature and life situation.

For the mother, wildness might be abandoning the laundry and running joyously out in the back yard to jump in the mud puddles with her children. For a painter, it may be covering herself with oils and rolling sensuously over her canvas. For another, it's gathering with her friends to dance naked around a fire and howl at the moon; for the old woman, it

1

could be staying up late so moonlight can fall upon her face as she rocks to and fro singing her soul's song.

She is the woman who feels she's had a good life, and is ready for more fun and wildness. She is the woman who has been healed from her past wounds and is now looking for the next step. She is the mother who says: I need time for fun, too. I can feed and clothe my children, and still let my wild nature run free. She is the artist and the entertainer. She is the working woman, the professional, trying hard to achieve or, just, survive. She allows herself to wonder where her wild, fun side has gone — and then allows herself to find out. A wild woman is all colors, nationalities, body types, ages and sexual preferences.

Woman's wildness is pure. It is a part of our essence, an unleashing of our desires, passions, a joyful part of ourselves, spontaneous and uncontrollable. It's our rage, our grief, our wholeness. It is the depth of that purity that gives our lives force and power. How do we let something so natural come out in such a processed world? We need this essential wildness so our hearts can continue to beat, so that we can be less tamed and controlled by the world around us. What is needed is a current image of what it is to be a wild woman. We can call on past mentors, but if we look around there are acts of courage and wildness everywhere: in our friends, our teachers, in the media, in ourselves. We are all forming and discovering who our wild woman is. She will continue to affect what is happening in our overprocessed, repressed environments.

Callie Khouri, screenwriter for the movie *Thelma and Louise*, said, "As a female movie-goer, I just got fed up with the passive role of women. They were never driving the story because they were never driving the car."[1] Wildness is driving the car. Isn't it time we stopped supporting the denial of our wildness and urged one another to move into the driver's seat, to ride that horse, speak our truth, have less guilt and more fun? Wildness is one more part of us that wants to be expressed. When books were being written in the 1970s and 1980s on how to express our anger, women first thought, "I can't let my anger out, something will happen to me, I'll get hurt. I can't be that bold or honest. Besides, no one will listen anyway." Yet, with practice, it became easier to express our anger in ways that were healthy. Now we need to find a way to express our natural exuberance.

In the last ten years I've heard women ask over and over again, "What has happened to that fun, wild, impassioned part of myself? I feel overworked, overdone, overresponsible, over "everything." I've lost my sexual desires, my passion for life, my creative drive. Even when I get a few hours or days to myself, it's hard to do anything exciting, anything fun. Sometimes I sit and wait for the energy to come, but by the time it does it's back to business as usual!" This is the suffering that women experience today. They feel as if life is passing them by. They want more, but are not sure where to find it.

For good reason. That natural wildness has been long hidden. In *Iron John*, Robert Bly writes, "Welcoming the Hairy Man is scary and risky and it requires a different form of courage."[2]

Welcoming the *deep female* can also be frightening. The *deep female* is more natural, less edited, less careful with words and thoughts. Feelings flow, they come and go. It's risky to even admit to this side of ourselves, for something forbidden and unacceptable may emerge — a primal desire may show itself to us. The wild woman may decide she needs more food, more sex, more of everything.

By not allowing this side of ourselves to be expressed we have grown out of balance. We have become a society of caretakers, dutiful daughters and wives, respectable, hard workers and successful professionals; nice, settled, safe. Many of us feel overworked, overresponsible, anxious, depressed, lost, unfulfilled and nonsexual. These are all symptoms of co-dependence. Robert Subby, author of *Co-Dependency an Emerging Issue*, believes co-dependency is "a condition that develops as the result of an individual's prolonged exposure to and practice of, a set of *oppressive rules* — rules which prevent the open expression of feeling, as well as the direct discussion of personal and interpersonal problems."[3]

Anne Wilson Schaef writes in *Co-Dependence Misunderstood — Mistreated*, "Co-dependents are supreme controllers. They believe they can and should be able to control everything.

As situations become progressively chaotic, co-dependents exert more and more controls. These attempts at control are, I think, the major cause of physical illness. They are so intent on taking care of others, keeping things going that they often develop stress-related functional or psychosomatic diseases. They develop headaches, backaches, respiratory, heart and gastrointestinal problems, and hypertension. Even cancer has been linked to the disease. Co-dependents also develop addictions (like eating disorders, hyperactivity, workaholism, over-spending) and they sometimes move into chemical addictions."[4]

Wildness can be an antidote for such stress-related diseases. The author of *Anatomy of An Illness*, Norman Cousins, wrote that when he was in the hospital suffering from a crippling and supposedly irreversible disease, he asked the doctors to bring in Marx Brothers' movies and *Candid Camera* clips, and he asked the nurses to read comic material to him. He discovered that laughter played a major role in his recovery.

Expressing our wildness is part of our healing. Instead of being so "in control," we can be free to lose control. Instead of tightening, we can loosen. We can expand our bodies and our souls. We can let out what frightens us: the uncontrollable.

The idea of women expressing their wildness, of being less controlled, scares people. No wonder. If women become wilder and more carefree (less caretaking), it would challenge the whole caretaking structure of our culture. This doesn't mean that we will be cruel or careless, but it does mean we will care more for our hearts, our souls, our bodies, our energy.

Mentioning the words "wild woman" sometimes incites intense emotion among people. I've heard people say, "What are you talking about? What do you mean? Wildness is dangerous; being out of control, self-destructive, like an addict? Don't you think we should be responsible, we should act our age?" They warn that something bad could happen to women who express their free, wild natures. When I heard such negative responses, I knew that our culture had taken something that is pure and beautiful and necessary for full womanhood, and had given it a bad name.

Susan Faludi writes in *Backlash, the Undeclared War Against Women* how the media colluded to manipulate words, stories, statistics and documents to give the words "feminism" and "feminist movement" negative meanings. One result was that women began to believe that if they admitted to being feminists, it meant they were extremists and man-haters.

Merlin Stone, author of *When God Was A Woman*, addressed the same issue in historical accounts of the Goddess, "Within descriptions of long-buried cities and temples, academic authors wrote of sexually active Goddesses as 'improper,' 'unbearably aggressive' or 'embarrassingly void of morals,' while male deities, who raped or seduced legendary numbers of women or nymphs were described as 'playful' or even admirably 'virile.' The women who followed the ancient sexual customs of the Goddess faith, known in their own language as sacred or holy women, were repeatedly referred to as 'ritual prostitutes.' "[5]

Feverish debates over the rules of women in current films have also led to some "female bashing." The hotly debated film, *Thelma and Louise*, had two friends riding across the desert in a turquoise convertible attempting to escape the police. Louise, played by Susan Sarandon, shoots and kills a man who was raping her friend. Thelma, played by Geena Davis, holds up a convenience store and they both blow up an oil tanker driven by an obnoxious macho male. At this point we have no doubt that these are wild women.

The cover of *Time* magazine reads "Gender Bender; a white-hot debate rages over whether *Thelma and Louise* celebrates liberated females, male bashers, or outlaws." The article stated, "What people sense, particularly in Davis' performance, is that she is getting off on her newly discovered taste and talent for gun-slinging outlawry. It's a kick, not so very different from, maybe part and parcel of, her newly discovered pleasure in sex. This is something nice girls — nice people, nice movies — are not supposed to own up to, let alone speak of humorously."[6] As the movie concludes, the women make their choice, kiss and hug each other, and drive off a desert cliff rather than submit to a system designed to take their new-found power away.

Yes, the actresses received flack, just as other women who played roles involving power and violence have. Linda

Hamilton in *Terminator 2* carried heavy brains, fire power and muscle to protect her son and the future of the planet. Kathleen Turner, in *V.I. Warshawski*, again using brains and muscle, protected the rights of a child she had befriended.

Violence expressed *by women* may not be to your liking, but the all-out expressiveness and particularly the wildness in *Thelma and Louise* calls out to us. "The violence I liked in a way," says Sarandon, "because it is not premeditated. It is primal, and it doesn't solve anything."[7] Being wild does not inevitably mean expressing rage through violence, but we cannot exclude this possibility.

Wild women have always been in our literature, thanks to the writings of Anais Nin, Alice Walker, Lillian Hellman and George Sand (Armandine Lucile Amore Dupin-Dudevaut) to name a few. Karen Brennan, author of the award-winning novel *Wild Desire* describes one of her characters:

> "Carolyn tosses her tennis racket into a green dumpster. It lands on a bum's head but doesn't wake him up. Rather the thud of the tennis racket makes the bum go deeper into a coma. Carolyn is wearing a cute little tennis tutu and pearls. Her white blonde hair is tied back with a pink ribbon. She is Biff's wife. She has thrown out her racket because she is sick to death of tennis and all the accouterments of tennis which she now considers hollow and unfulfilling. With this gesture — throwing the tennis racket into the green dumpster — she is starting a new life. A life with passion. Angrily, she pulls the pink ribbon from her white blonde hair and hurls it into the dumpster after the tennis racket. Then her shoes and socks and, what the hell, the tutu, the sleeveless tee shirt, the matching Christian Dior bra and panties. In the end, all she has on are pearls. I don't care, she says. I want some feeling mixed with a social consciousness in my life. Luckily it's not cold out. Nevertheless, some people report her to the police and before long the asylum truck comes to take her away."[8]

Perhaps, you're thinking that driving a car off a cliff or going to an insane asylum isn't your idea of fun. Yet, these books and movies excite us because they push the edge of the envelope.

For Carolyn, I cheer her on knowing that she's finally had it and is on her way to a new life. And, as Thelma and Louise drive across the desert at night, there's a sense of fulfillment for them. They know they have become more than they had been. They have made choices and these choices won't permit them to go back to their old ways of living. You may not choose to do what they have done, but maybe, like Carolyn, you're ready to throw all or part of your old ways into the garbage and let your wild side out.

Wildness is natural. Think of the great teacher, nature: the fierce storms, rushing rivers, erupting volcanoes, earthquakes, wild forests and animals. It is natural and healthy for our world to be untamed. Yet, so much human effort concentrates on taming and controlling nature. We restrain water in dams for electricity, we deplete the ozone layer, our lungs are robbed of oxygen by the destruction of our rain forests. Control is not negative; in fact, it can be a positive thing. But too much of anything can be destructive.

We, too, are suffering from that taming. True spirituality comes from letting go of control, knowing each moment that the spiritual force of the universe will take care of us. Many of us speak of faith and trusting, but if we examine our lives they are, for most of us, filled with issues of control: managing emotions, scheduling our days, negotiating relationships. Think about it. Is there any room in your day for an interruption, let alone an *eruption*?

What would your life be like if you really believed you were taken care of? If you believed some kind of spiritual force would be there for you whenever you needed it? I believe part of the journey back to that trust, back to our true selves and deep spirituality, is the expression of our wild nature.

The problem so many of us face is how to let go, how to trust? The more trauma, wounds and betrayal we experienced as young children, the more difficult (not impossible) it is for us to let go. The words "out of control" have frightening memories connected with them for many people. If you grew up in an out-of-control environment, perhaps with an alcoholic or mentally ill parent and/or suffered from physical and/or sexual abuse, then you would know how destructive loss of control can be. To survive as a child you would have sought control in your life, and are most likely still seeking it.

Even if you did not grow up in that kind of traumatic environment, you may have suffered from common societal and parental indoctrinations. I have heard women say they were too loud or too much; they were told to "act like a girl, be nice, you're too noisy, stop that, you'll embarrass me." Alice Miller writes in *For Your Own Good*, how children were horribly beaten for showing any exuberance at all.

So, do we stop here and agree that suppression began with our parents and their parents? Partly, yes, because there is much responsibility that belongs with past and present parenting. Yet, when I spoke to women about being wild, their fears seemed deeper than this lifetime. Do we, as many believe, carry the fear of the Goddess mutilations and witch burnings in our souls? Carl Jung would say this is part of our collective unconscious, that these horror stories were passed from generation to generation to form that consciousness.

Seventy-two-year-old archaeologist Marijas Gimbutas says the rapes and mutilations began three thousand years ago. The Goddess culture, not prepared for the brutality of the warriors from the north, were completely dominated. Later, in the 14th and 15th centuries, when it was feared that worship of the Goddess was still occurring, the persecution of the witches began. Women learned quickly to hide any sense of power, any sense of their feminine mystique.

This relatively recent history of three to four thousand years of persecution and repression continues to affect us all. We needn't look much further to find the basis for the fear of expressing anything but the culturally acceptable.

Arriving in the 20th century, we know that suffragettes seeking women's rights and fighting for the right to vote were seen as troublemakers for rallying in the streets and meeting halls. Again, in the 1960s, with the civil rights and feminist movements, women were seen as wild extremists, marching in the streets, urging peace and quality of race and sex. We were not asking for dominance, only equality. In the 1980s, with the suppressive Reagan and Bush governments taking us three giant steps backward, women's voices were muffled. Did we quiet down because we were shamed by the *"white male system,"* as Anne Wilson Schaef calls it, or were we taking time to focus on the internal?

In the 1970s and 1980s, I found my friends reading self-help books, such as Robin Norwood's *Women Who Love Too Much*, Melodie Beattie's *Co-Dependent No More*, *The Courage to Heal* by Laura Davis and Ellen Bass, and *You Can Heal Your Life* by Louise Hay. People began to look deeply within to heal the hurt and shame of the past. They were seeking ways to build self-esteem and end the suffering they felt inside. Literally, hundreds of books dealing with addiction were on the bookstands. For many people, addictions were a way to numb themselves, or have some fun or wild times: spending wildly, eating the most luscious desserts, drinking or drugging. However, for many, the escapes they relied on became the problems themselves. Now, there were no escapes. Through support groups and self-help books, women learned that what was needed was self-care. I, for one, didn't know what that meant, so people would say to me, "Get child care, take time off, take a bubble bath, go to a movie, eat out." Although some things I did made a difference, I found my life lacking a sense of liveliness. Some of my friends began to work so hard at taking care of themselves that they were exhausted by it.

I believe women have gotten tired of working so hard on themselves. That's when I began to hear women say, "Where's the fun in my life? When's the last time I did anything wild? I'm too tired to have sex, where's the passion in my life?" It's become necessary for us to find a way to put spirit back into our lives through creativity, fun and our own desires.

When I interviewed Virginia Satir for my book, *Women of Power*, she said it was important to focus on what someone wanted more of, rather than what they didn't have. "Look for the new possibilities," she said. I felt my new possibilities would come by allowing my spirit to permeate my life. Instead of trying so hard to get rid of my caretaking, overwork and seriousness, I began to listen to my wild heart and allow it to guide me. This led me to more fun and new possibilities within.

At least I knew *something* about having a good time. Though my family had its share of dysfunctions, we were still able to have fun and be ridiculous. We often performed theater for each other. One of our family traditions was yearly or biyearly trips to Disneyland and Knott's Berry Farm. We often took weekend trips exploring local areas. We had one neighbor who kept an immaculate yard, while ours was always lacking in perfection. He would hint that we should stay home more and work on the yard. He offered us the use of his mower, tools, etc. I can still remember the disapproval on that man's face as we would once again wave good-bye and set out on a weekend adventure.

When I began to look for the fun and spontaneity in people, I began to see more of it. I began to believe that healing could come from being wild, having more fun and, most importantly, that this was an essential and natural process for women. I began to incorporate more fun and wildness into my life, and to ask others to try things and tell me how it went. Friends and clients returned with some very interesting stories that teach and inspire. Here are some examples.

A very sophisticated and proper woman had been living with a half-finished deck for months. She had paid the contractor in advance, and now he felt no hurry to finish the job or return her phone calls. One day she walked into his office and asked him when the job would be done, but he refused to give her a straight answer. She surprised herself when she suddenly grabbed a valuable painting off his wall and ran out of his office with it, yelling that he'd have his painting when she had her deck. She was both shocked and exhilarated by her behavior. She admits to having stayed up half the night, afraid the police would come. They didn't, but the contractor and his work crew came and finished her job the next week.

Another woman, Jessie, had been practicing ways to take care of herself. One day I suggested that she do something a little wild this week, and come back and tell me how it felt. One morning, while her two children were playing, she dropped the laundry, put some music on, and began to dance with them. She laughed out loud as she danced with both her children. Because her children had never seen her play like that, they were frightened and began to cry. She stopped, gathered them together, and told them that it was O.K. for Mommy to play, too, and that maybe they could all dance together . . . and they did. She told me that they had lots of fun and that she felt refreshed inside. Then she cried, realizing she had never shared that kind of time with her own mother.

One of my friends who was tired of being single drove to her sacred mountain on a full-moon night. She got out of her car and shook her fists at the mountain and said, "Look, big, powerful clump of earth, I do a lot for you. Now, it's my turn. I've had it with being alone. I want someone in my life and I expect you to deliver." After she stomped around a bit, she drove back to town and stopped at the ice cream store for comfort. While making her selection, she suddenly heard this deep voice say, "I see you're a chocolate lover, too." She looked up and saw this dark haired, beautiful man standing there. He asked her if she'd care to walk around the town together. She agreed. Then when they were in a gazebo, he asked if she would dance with him. At first she felt embarrassed. Then, she said, "What the hell," and took his arms. They had a wonderful dance and later parted. She never saw him again, but was happy for their meeting. She sensed the mountain was telling her someone was on the way.

In each of these examples, risking being uninhibited made a difference in their days. What I have described may not be the way you would express your own wild nature and, after all, what is wild to one person may seem mild to another. Yet, it is important not to grade our wildness. We will each find what is natural as we explore this new territory.

We have both an inner and an outer wildness. Inside, we begin with being willing to listen to that uninhibited part of ourselves. What is each woman's wild nature like deep inside? Perhaps it is in the stillness when you're all alone, or when you hear the sound of your favorite singer and you find your body moving to the beat of the music. Fun, "forbidden," untamed feelings and fantasies may reveal themselves.

The author of *Wild Mind*, Natalie Goldberg, writes, "wild mind surrounds us. Western psychology calls wild mind the unconscious, but I think the unconscious is a limiting term. If it is true that we are all inter-penetrated and interconnected, then the wild mind includes mountains, rivers, Cadillacs, humidity, plains, emeralds, poverty, old streets in London, snow, and moon. A river and a tree are not unconscious. They are part of wild mind.

"Psychotherapy can help to bring you into wild mind, for you to learn to be comfortable there, rather than constantly grabbing a tidbit from the wild mind and shoving it into the conscious mind, thereby trying to get control of it. This is what Zen, too, asks you to do: to sit down in the middle of your wild mind. This is all about a loss of control. This is what falling in love is, too: a loss of control.

"Can you do this? Lose control and let wild mind take over? It is the best way to write. To live, too."[9]

When I've been with groups of women, I've encouraged them to listen to that inner wild side, to lose control, to ask themselves what would put spirit back in their lives, what is their most outrageous idea or fantasy? What kind of "wild and crazy" things would they like to do?

Some of the things I've heard women say (editing out the more pornographic, which I'll leave to your wild imagination) are:

- I'm going to quit my job and become a race car driver.

- I'm sick of watching my husband sit in front of the T.V. while I work and take care of the kids. I'll drop the kids at my Mom's and buy a ticket to Rio.

- I can't remember the last time I had good sex. I'm going to go out and find someone to have sex with, or maybe two or three people.

- I'm going to give away everything I own and become a bag lady.

- I want to tell my parents what I really think of them.

- I'd blow the head off my molester, only after torturing him the way he did me.

- I'll never clean the house and then I'll yell profanities at anyone who dares to make comments.

- I'm not going to class today. Maybe I'll sit outside, eat chocolates, and read movie magazines.

- I'd send Kevin Costner a nude photo of me and ask for a date.

- I want to run naked through the streets yelling "Fuck, Fuck, Fuck" and see what happens.

- I don't care if I'm forty years old. It's never too late to do what I want. I'm going to sign up for that acting class now.

- I think I'll trade in the station wagon for a convertible and drive across the desert.

Some of these desires may seem extreme to you. Good! That's the way it's supposed to be. When we've kept a part of ourselves chained up for so long, it's normal for that wildness to come out in bold, unsettling, noisy, rageful, rebellious, uncontrollable ways. It's time to free our minds from captivity.

Swiss psychoanalyst, Marie-Louise Von Franz, wrote of the unconscious, "the shadow usually contains values that are needed by the consciousness, but exist in a form that makes it difficult to integrate them into one's life."[10]

Integrating our inner liveliness and daring into our external lives is part of the challenge. So far we've spoken of letting out that inner wildness by listening to what we may have suppressed or denied for a long time. When we begin to practice external wildness by bringing these desires and actions into the world, we need to remember first that we're in charge and can choose where and when we want to be wild, and how wild we want to be. It's also important for us to realize that our wild side is only one part of us, and we do not have to let it consume our lives. However, when wildness has been ignored for too long and we first decide to tap into it, we may feel such joy that it may initially consume much of our time. And then, who knows, we may have such a good time that it will continue to be a larger and larger part of our lives.

When we move from the internal to the external, we need a healthy conscience to integrate our wild desires into our lives. I see a healthy conscience as a compassionate, wise, nurturing aspect of ourselves. It has integrity: a sense of what is right and wrong for us. It is a part of us that has developed over time, that has a code of ethics that we can live comfortably with. It is also a part of us that can embrace our wild side knowing that it is both needed and natural, but not the voice of an "internal oppressor" or controller.

The oppressor is a part of us that wants to keep things under control. If everything was out of control as a child, you would have fought for control in order to feel safe. You may also have been heavily controlled, and your spirit oppressed by your environment. This means you learned well how to control, and what being controlled is. That knowledge is still working for you. That's why most people need to control their lives, and why it is so difficult for them to let go. When control has been taken to the extreme, as it has for many of us, it becomes oppressive. That's why I feel (besides dealing with a suppressive society externally) we are living with this internal oppressor inside. Our oppressor will basically say "no" to anything that threatens to change, "no" to too many feelings, "no" to ideas that will sacrifice the security it knows and, of course, "no" to anything risky or wild. Its goal is to keep us under control, to not let us get out of hand.

How the healthy conscience deals with the controller or oppressor will be discussed in Chapter 3. You can always count on your oppressor to respond to wildness with something like, "Don't even consider doing that. What will people think? You're too tired, too young, too old. You'll look stupid. How dare you embarrass me." Our supportive conscience would most likely respond with, "I like your ideas. That sounds like fun. Let's see if we can do that. Good for you for coming up with this."

Your wild side may feel like moonbathing naked, or catching a plane to Paris and falling in love. It is at this point that your conscience may say, "Great, it's warm outside and there's a beautiful fall moon. Let's fix a picnic and bask in the light." Regarding Paris, you may evaluate the situation and say, "Instead of leaving tomorrow, let's get that great twenty-one-day deal, give your clients notice, and then go for it."

Perhaps, it seems that our spontaneity is being limited. But we can make momentary decisions so that it won't seem that any time has passed between our wild thought and action. Perhaps you'll see a beautiful woman or man walking down the street, and in a split second you know that you will reach out your hand and say, "You are beautiful to look at." Our minds work so rapidly that in most cases we don't even realize this sorting period has happened. Then, at other times, events are more thought out.

Our healthy conscience does oversee our choices. It can deter us from self-destructive behavior. Often our wild side wants to act out in destructive, rebellious or addictive ways. It's up to us to decide how much acting out is fun, versus what can ultimately be harmful. Self-destruction, like abuse of drugs, sex and spending, can be used to express wildness, but it is not the way to our true feminine wild side. It actually masks it. Addictions numb our true feelings and suppress our spirit. Drinking alcohol or taking drugs may have brought out a wild, uninhibited part of ourselves, yet, if we had expressed those feelings without "coating" our souls, we'd be more aware of what real spontaneity and fun are.

We can reach deep inside our psyches, giving ourselves approval to do what is natural to us, uninhibited by what others think. We can discover that fun, alive, vibrant part that has been buried by years of indoctrination. We can expand our bodies and minds, opening up to this hidden wellspring. At times, it's like being a child again, before we began to notice how people were reacting to us. It's letting our souls sing, our bodies feel passion and surges of sexual desire.

Wildness opens up the whole area of sexual fantasies, and whether or not you're going to act them out. It's surprising how many women, single or with partners, will say, "I just want to have sex. I want to have an affair. I want to know what it's like to feel passionate, to abandon myself, to be dripping with juice and feel sweat pouring off my body." When women begin sharing these feelings (and much more), the room heats up. We deserve to have these feelings and desires fulfilled, and it's up to us to work out how, or even if, we will meet these needs. Some will find ways to bring these feelings to a long-time partnership, to discover them alone, or develop a new friendship.

I spoke to a woman who said, "I followed my feelings, my wildness, and had an affair. I felt more alive, more beautiful, more empowered, more sexual than I had in years." Others, who have had affairs, may feel freedom for the moment, yet later regret their spontaneous wild acts. Each woman needs to find a way to be herself that may challenge old ways of thinking and being, but not test her core values. In some cases, an affair, no matter how empowering at the moment, in the long run could be destructive. Yet, for others, a walk on the wild side is what is needed in order to leave a passionless relationship.

I've heard people say, "If I let out my wildness, it could be dangerous." Yet, look at how dangerous we have been to ourselves. Observe, for example, the rise of stress-related, life-threatening diseases. Spontaneity can keep us safe and healthy. Often, it's the people who are exploring their wild sides who are the least dangerous to themselves. Again, whatever is suppressed will manifest itself in another form. If we are suppressing that spirit in us, it can sneak out in resentment, depression, rage toward a partner, friends, even our children. Then self-hatred, bitterness and hopelessness will follow.

We've become experts on suppression; now it's time to become authorities on the wild side. For support in my journey I have turned to women, present and past, who know about bringing spirit into their lives and those of others. History is filled with wild, bold women who risked and succeeded; who reigned, survived and flourished. We can turn to images of the Goddesses or the mystics, healers, social/political leaders, outlaws, artists and entertainers.

We have the Great Goddess Mother of Wild Animals, the erotic Goddesses of Lilith and Ishtar, and the Hindu Goddess Kali. We have mystics like Mother Theresa; the spiritual and psychological risk-takers Elizabeth Kubler-Ross and Virginia Satir; social activist Margaret Sanger; artist and civil rights leader Josephine Baker; dancer Isadora Duncan; painter and writer Georgia O'Keefe; singers Tina Turner and Madonna; writer Anais Nin; poet Sapphire; comedians Whoopi Goldberg and Judy Tanuda; performance artists Karen Finley and Holly Hughes. These women are pioneers, women who followed their instincts, ignoring the taboos of society. We can call upon their stories and their courage.

I have chosen only a few women here, some of the most famous, public women. Yet, if you look around, you will find your mentors in each other.

My friend, Susan King, is one of my wild mentors. She suggested I call this book *A Whistling Woman Is Up to No Good* because of a story she told me. In the 1950s, she had gone to visit her husband's parents in Kentucky. A few days into the trip, her husband came up to her and asked her to please stop whistling. Apparently, his parents found a whistling woman inappropriate and offensive. In fact, it showed she wasn't in her proper place. She was too free-spirited, uncontrollable, and even up to something — probably trouble — or having a good time? Well, Susan says she stayed in that marriage too long. She is today one of the wildest women I know. She is so unaffected by what others think, and so willing to be herself in and out of public, that for a long time I assumed she was simply from another planet.

Since childhood, Susan has had a great love for Native American heritage, so at one time she was able to purchase a beautiful feathered headdress. Now, when the mood hits, she'll adorn the headdress and drive down to the local and very popular bookstore, walk into the children's section and read children's books. I've asked her what people say or do. What surprises me is that people don't do or say anything, except a few children who wander over to talk to her. I've made a promise to myself to pack a squirt gun, dress up as Annie Oakley, and join her one evening. There's something exhilarating about doing the unusual.

Friends can be a great source of encouragement and stimulation for wildness. It's catching. It's like teenage girls who travel in groups to boost their courage and have more fun. I love gatherings with groups of my women friends, playing dress-up together like we did as children, parading in front of the mirror, pretending to be our favorite movie stars. Then we'll go out on the town. Other times we'll build a fire and dance with total abandonment. Then there are evenings we'll sit and share our deepest feelings and desires.

At times, our wild natures are expressed alone. Sometimes, in meditation, people will feel inner passion for life growing within them. I've often wondered what goes on in the minds and bodies of Indian gurus who sit giggling as they meditate. They're probably experiencing uninhibited blissful feelings.

Then there are times when we're alone and experience our deep, wild natures in ways that only we know about: our play, movement noise, our art. Or when we're alone, and dead tired. It's times like these that we can let our minds run free, instead of thinking of all the things we have to do or should do, or what's wrong with us. We can look out the window at a cloud and notice what that cloud reminds us of, and then follow that thought and then the next thought. It's also these still times when creative inspiration can come to us. As Natalie Goldberg would say, let your mind lose control.

There will also be those of us who bring our wildness into our intimate relationships, sex, our friendships, our parenting, our careers and work. Exploring our wild natures will affect all of these areas in positive ways.

I also know that listening to our hearts, and what is wild within, is not always comfortable. Many of us want to listen to our wild hearts only as long as we don't have to step on someone's toes, inconvenience anyone, or maybe change our lives. It is frightening to think we might move beyond traditional boundaries and the approval of others. Yet, it is more frightening to think that if we continue to suppress this natural part of ourselves, we could shatter our chances at a full life. I wonder if there doesn't come a time in our lives (and I mean at any age) when we're either going to take the leap to have more fun and be ourselves, or turn in our chips and become old in spirit.

Some of you may already be experiencing your wild nature: that fun, bold, uncensored part of yourself. Others may not even have a sense of what their wild side is like. No matter where you are in this adventure, you can still explore further. You can take steps toward expressing this hidden part of yourself. Like anything, it does not have to happen all at once. We can move at whatever speed we choose, as we invite in more of our wild nature.

Wildness is that deep, full, uninhibited part of us. We need fewer controls in our world. We could use some irreverence toward some of what we see around us. We need bold thoughts and actions, more joy, more fierceness, more untamed people and environments. We can invite in our wild natures, so that when we reflect on our days we'll know how honest they have been, and how alive we have become. We can start listening to our wild hearts — they have been ignored for too long. We can live free, uncensored lives. Yes, *you* can become a wild, wild woman.

Chapter 1 Footnotes

[1] Simpson, Janice E. "Moving Into the Driver's Seat." *Time,* June 24, 1991, 55.

[2] Bly, Robert. *Iron John: A Book About Men.* New York: Addison Wesley Publishing Company, Inc., 1990, 52.

[3] Subby, Robert. *Co-Dependency: An Emerging Issue.* Health Communication, 1984, 26.

[4] Schaef, Anne Wilson. *Co-Dependence: Misunderstood — Mistreated.* San Francisco: Harper & Row, 1986, 54-56.

[5] Stone, Merlin. *When God Was A Woman.* New York: Harcourt Brace Jovanovich, 1978.

[6] Schickel, Richard. "Gender Bender; a white-hot debate rages over whether *Thelma & Louise* celebrates liberated females, male bashers or outlaws." *Time,* June 24, 1991, 56.

[7] *Ibid.,* 56.

[8] Brennan, Karen. *Wild Desires.* Amherst, MA: The University of Massachusetts Press, 1991, 56-60.

[9] Goldberg, Natalie. *Wild Mind.* New York: Bantam Books, 1990, 32-33.

[10] Von Franz, Marie-Louise. "The Realization of the Shadow in Dreams." *Meeting the Shadow: The Hidden Power of the Darkside of Human Nature.* Los Angeles: Jeremy P. Tarcher, 1990, 36.

2
Oh Wild Woman
Where Have You Gone?

I donned the black onyx cross embodied in silver leaves with a diamond at the center. For some unknown reason, I had been afraid of this cross when it had first been given to me. It was a gift from a friend who lived on a reservation I frequented. Because the cross unsettled me, I had sent it to my friend in New York knowing he loves crosses (hoping to dispose of it). But it always came back. Finally, neither he nor I heard any more from it.

A few years later my husband, Chris, waltzed into the room saying exuberantly, "Look what I found." I looked at the cross in horror. I believe, now, that I knew it was the key to my hidden side, the part more traditionally entitled the shadow which is associated with our negative emotions. I was not interested in pursuing what could be lurking *there*. Projecting my fears upon this cross, I even went so far as to think it might carry some kind of danger for those who wore it. Seeing the look on my face, Chris said, "I'll put it somewhere for safe-keeping." I said, "How about the ocean?" Several years later I discovered its hiding place, and it was only then that I placed it around my neck.

Since the cross was first given to me, I have spent much time facing who I am and what emotions lie within. It is amazing how looking inward at one's shadow can also change your external sight. I now see this cross as a priceless gift from an ancient woman of wisdom.

My friend Trish arrived from Australia, a director, singer and healer *extraordinaire*. Her wild woman story inspired me. I knew that I had not yet entered in my life the place where she lived. She was able to have faith in the moment. "Well if it's meant to be, it will happen," she'd say. She was led to live and work with the Sioux Native Americans for part of her journey, and this is where she learned some of her healing skills. She said things only got complicated when the seventy-five-year-old Chief wanted to marry her. She decided it was time to pack up and leave. Oh, wild woman!

During her visit, we picked up my little girl, Lily, at day care and began driving the windy coastal road toward home. Suddenly, Trish grabbed the back of my neck and said, "What is it, what is it?" I went into shock and Lily started screaming, "Stop hurting my mama." Trish waved her hand over Lily and my daughter immediately went to sleep. I was still trying to make the curves while this bulldog had her hands on the back of my neck. Finally, it occurred to me that I could tell her to let go, and she did. When we got home both Lily and I became terribly ill. I experienced the worst flu symptoms. Trish said, "Oh, it is only die off," and I said, "Thanks a lot," as I hung over the toilet seat. Lily developed a fever and cough. Later, as I felt some relief but still could not move much, I asked Trish to check on Lily's fever. She did. As soon as she separated what she calls our ethereal bodies, Lily perked up and the fever left.

I had no idea what the whole thing had been about until a week later when I was writing the "Protect the Wild" chapter. I was taken back in time to twenty years earlier, when a man came up behind me and held a knife to my throat. He asked me to take my coat off and, frozen with fear, I began to cooperate. I prayed aloud and asked him to please not do this. Suddenly, he and the knife were gone. I looked back to see him running in one direction, and I began running in the other.

I realize now that I had very few feelings about this encounter at the time. Any grief and rage I felt had been suppressed. I met with the police and they said my assailant fit the description of a man who had been raping women in the area. After talking to them, I went back to work, and I told very few people about the incident.

But today it is different; I remembered this terrifying experience and felt what I could not feel then. I started screaming and screaming and screaming. Fortunately, I was staying at a studio isolated on a thousand acres. Then the screaming took me back to a time in junior high school when I stood out and was very popular. I was in the pep squad and was dating the most popular boy in school. My best friend, a redheaded beauty, was the leader of the clique of girls at the school I was going to. One day she just stopped talking to me — and so did everybody else. I can still feel the pain of that loneliness. There was a point when I thought I couldn't live through it a moment longer. Then, just as abruptly as the alienation had happened, so then did the invitation to rejoin the group. But I had learned my lesson well: do not stand out or shine too much. No wonder public speaking always made me feel endangered. It was as if I could feel that knife at my throat in one way or another.

What I had kept hidden for so long finally had a chance to surface. It has been both painful and freeing, feeling what I had kept from myself for so long. The shadow needs to be seen or else it will cause us pain in other ways. For example, it can cause someone to repress who she is, to rage unsuspecting at loved ones, or be jealous of a friend's success. Many of us have repressed our anger, competitiveness and forbidden desires for too long. Often women do not like to admit to their neediness or weakness. As long as these feelings are repressed, when they finally surface they can come out sideways instead of straight on. But, when allowed to be a part of our daily life by listening and dealing with these emotions, their power over us is lessened. A friend of mine was never jealous of anyone or anything. I always assumed she was an evolved spirit. Then one full-moon night we were to meet for a solstice gathering at a beautiful million dollar home I was housesitting. Due to miscommunication and my broken alarm clock, I made her wait for close to an hour. She arrived, hah! She exploded through the door furious at me for holding her up. Then she started screaming, "Why do you get to housesit such a beautiful home and why don't I have these kinds of friends and a husband to take care of my child while I write?" So much for lack of envy. By then, I was angry too, so we had a blowout fight. I handed her a towel and said, "Why don't you go out to the hot tub." Meanwhile, I was moving around the house, feeling guilty and abandoned, knowing that she would certainly prefer being by herself.

Then I heard the door open and she said, "Aren't you coming out?" She was feeling sad that her life was scheduled so tightly that one hour would make such a difference. She was also afraid she had pushed me away. We talked and I told her I felt so bad for screwing up, I assumed she would rather be alone. I too had felt lost. Lately, I told her, all it would take for me to feel abandoned was somebody walking into the other room for a glass of water. We laughed and agreed that tonight Persephone, the Goddess of the underworld, would be proud of us as we began our winter's journey with a bang. Even in the pain, we felt some kind of freedom to at least know what we were looking at.

The Hidden Shadow Self

If you do not know what you want from life and have not had the freedom to discover who you really are, then your wild woman has become a part of your shadow self. This hidden self often has qualities that are not acceptable to whom we think we are or should be, and this is why we try to suppress them. They are often qualities that we have learned are alien to our oppressive society. The shadow can hold murderous rage, excessive greed, jealousy and hatred. It can also hold, for many women, the artist, her sexuality and her power.

If women have been abused and believe that they are not good enough, if they have been told repeatedly that what they feel is wrong, then to survive they will banish parts of themselves to an inner cave. We quickly learn who has the power, and what has to be done with ours. For example, has there ever been a woman president or vice president? How many supreme court justices, governors and congresswomen are there? Only in the past sixty years or less have we seen women professionals. Unfortunately, many of the women in the earlier times, and some even today, have had to suppress their naturalness to become part of the "white male system." Women learn quickly what happens when we seek to unleash our passion. Men do not like us as well, even some other women seem threatened. We are told we are "too much" and could suffer harm due to "stretching our wings." So, we hide our power. Because of this, the anger builds and it is turned inward, creating tremendous fear, despair, or destructive behavior such as addiction to food, chemicals or people. It could also be unexpectedly turned outward: "Oh no, I screamed at my co-worker, mate or child."

The only way to turn this cycle around is to enter one's cave deep within and explore what is there. The rage, excessive ambition or greed can all be seen differently when faced. Our wild woman can guide us in our journey underground, and then back to the surface where we can see things more clearly.

According to Jungian analyst Clarisa Pinkola Estés, "The shadow also can contain the divine, the luscious, beautiful, and powerful aspects of personhood. For women especially, the shadow almost always contains very fine aspects of being that are forbidden, or given little support by her culture. At the bottom of the well in the psyches of too many women lies the visionary creator, the astute truth-teller, the far-seer, the one who can speak well of herself without denigration, who can face herself without cringing, who works to perfect her craft. The positive impulses in shadow for women in our culture most often revolve around permission for the creation of a hand-made life."[1]

Looking at things symbolically, we could say that the struggle we are experiencing today, between our feelings and whether or not we are going to listen to them, is reflected in our culture. Because this fear of the feminine is with us today, it leads people to assume things have always been this way. Fortunately, due to the work of contemporary anthropologists, archaeologists and historians, this theory has been disproved.

Patriarchy is a relatively new system. Monica Sjoo and Barbara Mor, authors of *The Great Cosmic Mother*, believe the original Goddess religion influenced culture for at least thirty thousand years. Gloria Feman Orenstein, author of *Reflowering of the Goddess*, states, "A global view is very much a part of the perceptions of Goddess as life energy everywhere and has been one of the major facets of the philosophy associated with women's spirituality. The DNA mitochondrial research of biochemist Allen C. Wilson, has extrapolated all human ancestral lives back to a single mother, probably living in Africa over 200,000 years ago. It seems we are one family."[2]

World-renowned archaeologist, Marija Gimbutas, writes, "the culture called Old Europe was characterized by a dominance of woman in society and worship of a Goddess incarnating the creative principal as Source and Giver of All. In this culture the male element, man and animal, represented spontaneous and life-stimulating — but not life generating — powers."[3] Gimbutas also agrees with Riane Eisler, author of *The Chalice and the Blade*, that there was more of a "gylany" which is a term Eisler used to describe "an alternative to a system based on the rank of half of humanity over the other."[4] This would exclude a strictly matriarchal or patriarchal society. Gimbutas has been able to make discoveries dating back as far as 6000 B.C. in Old Europe, where people lived in peace surrounded by beautiful, nourishing gardens. No evidence or need for walls or forts were discovered. Trade routes from one community to the other show how communities interacted in peace. Because these people were bonded to the earth, they did what was natural, what was free and wild. Monica Sjoo and Barbara Mor write, "Sacred circles made with stones were found in the deep Palaeolithic caves, and in them the traces of human feet that danced around and around. Cave paintings show the shaman dancing in animal skins and antler headdress; the foot marks on the cave floors reveal generations of ritual dancing by all; women, men, children. Dancing to — and with — the spirits of the animals is the most ancient human ceremony that we know."[5]

Many of the Native American tribes of this country had or have similar behaviors and beliefs. The women are worshipped and protected as the creators of life. Kenny, a Native American man of wisdom, whose Lummi tribe has been able to restore their matriarchal and spiritual practices, told a group of us that "woman is the only one who can create the miracle of life. In our culture the lineage is passed down through the woman's name and the child spends the first two years mostly with the mother learning from her. Eighty percent of what a child learns is learned in the first two years of life, after that it is left to the child's inborn integrity."

Gimbutas believes that the invasion of the Indo-Europeans into Old Europe occurred around three thousand years ago. When the suppression came, it came in ruthless and never-to-be-forgotten ways. Rapes, tortures, mutilations and slavery were part of the tactics used to repress and overpower the ancient and "threatening" religion of the Goddess. Historian Merlin Stone believes Goddess worship "was not totally suppressed until the time of the Christian Emperors of Rome and Byzantium who closed down the last temples in about 500 A.D."[6] After these times, the patriarchal system, at least in Indo-European civilizations, was dominant. Almost all leaders, rulers, professionals and artists were men. Patriarchy brought a system of dominance of one group over another; a male dominance over the Goddess religions and those with less warring power. Today, patriarchy means much the same. Yet women who have dulled their feelings can be just as dominating and ruthless as any other member of the system, and men in positions of lower financial standing or authority can be just as abused.

However, this need to destroy and dominate was a global phenomenon. The United States was no exception, events happened. Three examples of this would be when Columbus discovered America and Native Americans were seen as uneducated savages, when blacks were transported here as slaves, and when the Japanese citizens were torn out of their homes and put in prison camps during World War II. In these three holocausts, nations were slaughtered, millions of people were put into slavery and separated from their families. In a desire to "civilize" Native Americans, the children were ripped from their parents' arms and sent to schools far from home. Many were beaten and their mouths were washed out with soap if they spoke their tribal language. They would cry out for their mothers at night, but no one would come. Many died of sickness, just because they could not live in such a world.

"Wild Indians" were seen as dangerous people needing to be controlled. "Wild women are also viewed as dangerous and in need of control."

The fear and disrespect of the feminine is part of the patriarchal system. It emanates from a fear of one's own feelings. Feelings are generally seen as the feminine in modern psychology, and the male-dominated system has no room for them. After all, feelings can lead one astray and result in loss of control or unreasonable reactions. Feelings can be powerful enough to destroy nations or dominate others. This can also work in reverse. If one really felt the affects of one's actions, such as suppressing a race, hitting a child or allowing starvation, most could not continue to live with the internal conflict. As it is, people continue to ignore these feelings and end up with heart attacks or other life-threatening diseases. As stated, beginning three thousand years ago, the fear of the female was reflected through the brutality that followed; the worldwide Goddess mutilations and domination of anything indigenous or natural. Then, through Christianity, a strong male-dominated system, this suppression was institutionalized by presenting the female, Eve, as the one who forced us out of the Garden of Eden. Woman was made to appear as the culprit who stole our innocence and led us into the challenges and pains that followed. Yet, in truth, it was the warriors from the north who came down upon the Goddess indigenous cultures that robbed those civilizations of the peace they knew.

Later, when it was feared that the Goddess religion might be rising again, the witch hunts were started. Starhawk writes in *The Spiral Dance* that persecution began slowly in the 12th and 13th centuries, and came full force in 1484 when the Papal Bull, Innocent VIII, sent the forces of the Inquisition after the old religion. "The persecution was most strongly directed against women: an estimated 9 million witches were executed, 80% were women, including children and young girls, who were believed to inherit the 'evil' from their mothers."[7] Women were tortured and burned at the stake for petting a cat, being mentally ill, or offending others with their beauty. This offered people an opportunity to rid themselves of anyone they did not like or were merely threatened by. These persecutions, on a global scale, lasted hundreds of years, and made women learn to hide their power and any sense of the feminine mystic.

In the 19th and 20th centuries, women who had the courage to fight for the right to vote were arrested. The suffragettes protested these arrests through hunger strikes and were cruelly force-fed in prison. At this same time, all women, particularly women of color, were working for substandard wages. Many still do today.

The women involved in the feminist movement of the 1960s were fighting for equal rights, not dominance. They were labelled extremists and man-haters. Susan Faludi, author of *Backlash*, argues, "Anytime women have tried to loosen their corsets and breathe more freely, they met with suffocating counter attack. In the 1980s, this backlash surfaced in the White House, the courts, Hollywood, and above all, the mass media whose collective message to women went something like this; feminism is your worst enemy, all this freedom is making you miserable, unmarriageable, infertile, unstable. Go home, bake a cake, quit pounding on the doors of public life and all your troubles will go away."[8]

As the women's movement provided more opportunities for women in the workplace, there was little simultaneous lessening of women's traditional responsibilities. Many women were still the caretakers. There is that old belief that if we do it right, work hard enough and are controllable, maybe we will survive. The problem is that surviving is not good enough for women today.

We have learned this suppressive survival behavior from one another, and from a society that expects it. Children have learned how to treat themselves and others by observing their parents or influential adults. Children observe how their parents do not trust their own feelings. When a child talks about how she or he feels, their feelings are invalidated. At a young age, who are you going to trust: your perceptions or what your parents say? For survival, a child will choose to believe a parent, because they need to believe so desperately that their parents are trustworthy. Many children also learn to numb their feelings completely as the result of physical, sexual or emotional abuse.

Female children learn passive behavior by watching their parents play out traditional sex roles. Collette Dowling brought this out into the open in *The Cinderella Complex*. She wrote in 1981 that women secretly want to be saved. "We may not always recognize it . . ., but it exists in all of us, emerging when we least expect it, permeating our dreams, dampening our ambitions. It's possible that woman's wish to be saved goes back to the days of cave living, when man's greater physical strength was needed to protect mothers and children from the wild. But such a wish is no longer appropriate or constructive. We do not need to be saved."[9] Yet, today, women are still staying with their abusive husbands out of fear of not being able to support themselves or their children, a fear also seen in the battered woman's syndrome.

The Department of Labor reports that women's earnings have increased by an average of one cent a year for the past five years. In 1992, women earned an average of seventy-four cents for every dollar earned by men. Many women, especially single mothers, are expected to pay for the child care and housekeeping expenses which lowers their average wages even further. This is another expression of our increasingly repressive society. Not only is the right to earn equal pay a joke, but the right of women to control their own bodies is at stake. Women and men both live with increased taxes and controls. Every time you turn around, somebody wants to know your social security number.

These outer imbalances we experience daily are reflected internally and affect us physically, mentally, emotionally and spiritually. If we are unaware of our wild woman we may ignore physical symptoms, leaving our bodies vulnerable to serious illness. It can take something so extreme as a panic attack, a breast lump or a positive pap smear to make us listen to what our bodies are saying.

The New Bodies Ourselves states, "We squelch the fight-or-flight response over and over again in the course of a single day. It is an increasingly accepted theory that years of having to discharge the body's stress response can damage the body's immune (disease-fighting) system and result in many different kinds of ill health. Possible long-term consequences of living with too much stress are ulcers, high blood pressure, higher risk of coronary heart disease, rheumatoid arthritis, and cancer."[10] Medical literature has also linked multiple sclerosis and mitral valve syndrome to stress — most often in women. The authors of *The New Bodies Ourselves* believe illness is caused by the stress of single parenting, low pay, women's abilities being stilted in the workplace, and sexual harassment and abuse. Stress-related diseases can also be avoided by letting go of control. Stop trying to hold it all together and trust that some unique power can handle what we can't. If possible, take time for yourself. If we are less controlling, our personal health will improve. We'll carry less tension, less holding in the body. Maybe even make more noise, shout, fill the room with laughter, say inappropriate things and not worry about it.

There has been an epidemic rise in breast cancer. Bernie Siegel, M.D., author of *Love, Miracles, and Magic*, said that one of his patients would rather suffer cancer than tell her family "no." His studies showed that patients most likely to survive were those who appeared to have more difficult dispositions; they would not just go along with doctors' orders. They demanded answers to their questions, and would not accept traditional procedures. In other words, they stopped people-pleasing and demanded that others meet *their* needs.

Paying attention to our bodies — how much food, rest, exercise, touch and fun we need — means being aware of how we feel, and doing something about it. Unfortunately, many people are too busy or too addicted to food, drugs, shopping and work to notice how they feel, so the shadow thrives.

Our hidden self can be expressed emotionally in resentment, rage, bitterness, guilt, manipulation, envy, jealousy. Taken further we can experience self-destructive, homicidal, even suicidal behavior. That lurking shadow is more than willing to take over. We don't have to feel ashamed of these feelings. This is a natural response to captivity. It is as if we have become the prison guards to ourselves, even though we know society has encouraged this controlled behavior since infancy.

When women cannot face their feelings, or their "wild woman" is being suppressed, they can suffer anxiety or depression. "Women face a one-in-four chance of having a bout of severe depression during their lifetime. The odds of it striking are greatest between ages 25 and 44," according to Dareel Regier, M.D., who heads the division of clinical research at the National Institute of Mental Health. He continues, "Truly depressed people lose interest or pleasure in all or almost all of their normal activities for at least two weeks, and also have at least four of the following symptoms: change in appetite, significant weight loss or gain, insomnia or sleeping too much, bodily agitation or sluggishness, loss of energy, fatigue, feelings of worthlessness or self-reproach, diminished ability to think, concentrate, make decisions, thoughts of wanting to die, or actual plans to commit suicide."[11]

Consider what is said here. This is one-in-four women that have sought help for depression, not those who have not; this is what many women live with — what Thoreau described long ago as that "quiet desperation."

In truth, anxiety disorder sufferers far too often keep their troubles to themselves, no matter how tense and panicky they feel. More than three-quarters of those with serious anxiety problems never seek treatment, preferring to simply avoid worrisome situations, to settle their nerve with alcohol, or to suffer in silence. The results of the 1987 National Institute of Mental Health survey reveals that women are twice as likely to suffer from anxiety as men. They also stated that anxiety disorder is the nation's most common psychiatric diagnosis.

Combined with this is how easily our thinking can become distorted and negative. Because we are suffering inside, we focus on the ugliness, not the beauty, in the world. It is hard to figure out what comes first. Is what we are thinking affecting how we feel, or is our emotional and physical state leading us to think negative thoughts about ourselves or others? Since we are holistic beings, it is generally the combination.

Carl Jung believed that what lies buried within us becomes our shadow, a part of us that we feel is no longer safe for us or others to see. "This confrontation (with the shadow) is the first test of courage on the inner way, a test sufficient to frighten off most people, for the meeting with ourselves belongs to the more unpleasant things which can be avoided so long as we can project everything negative into the environment."[12]

I am not proposing that all this suffering is caused by our being out of touch with our "wild woman," but if we are not dealing with our feelings, our shadow life will be strong and our "wild woman" will remain painfully hidden.

In individuals we see such projections. Consider what was happening in one woman's life. Alice, a highly intelligent woman, was in the habit of breaking into sudden rages and projecting blame onto co-workers and her family. She was fired from several jobs and finally unable to get work. Her parents encouraged her to seek therapy. In therapy, she insisted that she was a "good person" and would never do anything wrong. She exclaimed that her boss was evil and so were her co-workers.

When her therapist asked her about her family members, she said that her sister had always been evil. Even the mention of her sister's name heightened her emotional state. When the therapist introduced the idea that Alice might feel that there was something evil about herself, Alice flew into a rage and left the office. She was being controlled by a strong, disowned part of herself. There were traumatic events so difficult for her to face that they had become a part of her hidden self. In order to know freedom, she would someday need to look at what was hiding within.

We are seeing this kind of projection everywhere: from gang and drug warfare, wars, child abuse, pollution of the environment, loss of hope, and blaming others rather than looking at our part of an event.

When the unconscious is not dealt with and the pain grows stronger, realities collide and dangerous, explosive feelings emerge. Look what is happening today — a rise in homicides by women, and women joining organizations such as the Ku Klux Klan, even though such groups are led by men and are anti-feminist.

"Whether they are Christian Identity church members, neo-Nazis, skin-heads, 'survivalists,' or white supremist tax protectors, their leadership without exception is male. The women insiders suggest proportions of 25% to 33% tend to be wives and girlfriends of male members."[13] It is still not uncommon to see women defending a perpetrator against other women, such as mothers whose children have been molested or female employees defending their boss on a sexual harassment charge. These women cannot face their own wounds, and certainly not those of others.

Professor Anita Hill, who accused Supreme Court Justice Clarence Thomas of sexual harassment, says, "The response to my Senate Judiciary Committee testimony has been heartwarming and heart-wrenching. In learning that I am not alone in experiencing harassment, I am also learning that there are far too many women who have experienced a range of inexcusable and illegal activities — from sexist jokes to sexual assault on the job. It occurs today at an alarming rate. Statistics show that anywhere between 42 and 90 percent of women will experience some form of harassment during their employed lives."[14] Resentment, rage, fear and shame are appropriate feelings as a result of these situations being shoved under the rug. The important thing is for us not to make it O.K., and to avoid self-destructive behavior in coping with our feelings. Strike out effectively.

One of the more positive things going on today is the exposure of women's' shadows in current films. How can we forget Dolly Parton, Lily Tomlin and Jane Fonda lashing out in the film *9 to 5*? Thank you Shirley MacLaine for your recent roles, both outrageous and real, and your wild, uncensored books. Thank you Callie Khouri for *Thelma and Louise* and Penny Marshall for *A League of Their Own* where women experience becoming their full selves.

Where movies are less available, cultures such as the Balinese bring out the conflict of good and evil with their festivals. They have as many as five to twenty festivals per month, using dance and puppets as part of their performances. "These religious rites and festivals guide the Balinese from birth to death and into the world thereafter. They provide the cohesive forces within the family unit and form the basis of a village community."[15]

Anthropologist Margaret Mead wrote, "The arts, especially music, dancing, and the theater, were enormously developed, and a great part of the time people whose remote dream-like behavior included a great capacity for almost endless untiring activity was spent in preparing for one dramatic ceremonial after another."[16]

Mead saw an orderly society in the South Pacific, a place where nature was respected and a child would never be hit out of fear of wounding her or his spirit. What she saw was the effect of allowing the unconscious to be conscious. We are well aware of what life can be like when the unconscious is ignored.

As Jung wrote, facing one's shadow can be a frightening prospect. However, you may want to ask yourself how it can show up in your life anyway as unbridled ambition, screaming at your partner or children, or addiction. These behaviors can be dealt with positively when brought to consciousness. Being ambitious is a positive quality as long as it is not running your life, as long as you choose how much you want to work and how you treat others. If you find yourself screaming at others who are not really the source of your anger, you can stop to examine whom or what you are really angry at — someone at work, someone from your past, too much responsibility? Looking at these feelings are less painful, in the long run, than what you are already living with. Sometimes, looking at something we do not like about ourselves is like getting a tooth pulled. What a relief to finally look within, grieve, and move on.

Once you begin to face these feelings, you will also become increasingly aware of the wild woman within. When she surfaces, she can be part of discovering how to handle your frustrations about life. She will show you more about the depth of your soul, giving you the courage to face yourself because, after all, she's been part of the hidden self.

The shadow is not something we want to get rid of completely, nor is there a chance that this will happen. It would be like having the sun without the moon and stars, or Anais Nin without moonbathing.

In Book VII of *Plato's Republic*, Plato presents an image of a dark cave where people have been chained since childhood. They are unable to move in order to see one another. A fire is blazing somewhere in the cave behind them. "Like ourselves, they see only their own shadows or the shadows of one another, which the fire throws on the opposite wall of the cave." Plato continues, "Like many they see only the appearance of material things, not what their true natures are."[17]

When the prisoners are freed and ascend into the real world, it takes them a while to figure out which is real: the shadows or what they see before them. Plato saw the ascent of the soul into the light as that of moving into the intellectual world, and the last to come into that world is the knowledge of good. But once that was seen, his future rulers would hurry to ascend further and further into the higher world and not want to deal with human affairs.

Plato saw a place for this world of the shadow. His future rulers would not be allowed to remain in the upper world. "They must be made to descend again among the prisoners in the den and partake of their labors and honors, whether they are worth having or not."[18] He saw the possibility that if his rulers lived only in the world of light, they would lose touch with their shadow. This would be a danger to their ability to be compassionate and worthy rulers. As Elizabeth Kübler-Ross says, "If we cannot face our own Hitler within, then we cannot know our Mother Theresa."

When released, our wild woman has the courage to ascend from the cave, and then aid us in descending back into our hidden self when necessary. She has lived in the shadows for so long, she can clearly navigate in the underworld. You may be jealous and angry with your workmate for doing less work than you — constantly reading a magazine and taking longer and longer lunches. Consequently, you drive yourself in order to get the work done. Being more in touch with your wild woman, you choose to talk with him about how you are feeling. He tells you that the work is getting done, and it is none of your business how much he works. Instead of pouring a pan of cold water over his head, you inform him that as his workmate, you are doing more than your share and would like to see this situation change. In so many words, he lets you know that the current arrangement is working out fine with him.

As you drive home, the anger begins to build. Later that night you suddenly get an image of your father sitting around drinking, while your mother brought home the money, took care of the house, and catered to your father's demands. You had always felt jealous of the time he took from you. Your wild woman leads you into your unconscious, and you feel this red-hot flame of jealousy and rage that you let loose by pounding on your bed and screaming through the house. At midnight you are at the gym working out. You get images of what you would like to have done to your father and what you would like to do to this guy at work.

By morning you are feeling tired but great! Your workmate is even less annoying to you. You packed a lunch for yourself that day and enjoyed the sun as you took a longer-than-usual lunchtime. The rest of the week you found it fun and relaxing to go to the gym during your lunch break. You are getting your share of the work done, and feeling better about yourself. After a few weeks, your workmate, Mr. Magazine, asks you how *we* plan to get this job done on time. You suggest that he do his share, and you will do yours. Then everything will get done. Otherwise, you both will be fired. Of course, there is a strong element of risk here. If he does not do his share, you will suffer too. But you have decided you would rather risk losing your job than living the way you have been. Miraculously, he begins to work more hours and you both find it enjoyable to exchange ideas. This is an example of your wild woman taking you into the depths of your fear and rage, and back up again with a creative and effective response to your problem.

Chapter 2 Footnotes

[1]   Estés, Clarisa Pinkola. *Women Who Run With The Wolves.* New York: Ballantine Books, 1992, 236.

[2]   Orenstein, Gloria Feman. *The Reflowering of the Goddess.* Tarrytown, NY: PPI UK, 1990.

[3]   Gimbutas, Marija. *The Goddesses and Gods of Old Europe — 6500-3500 B.C.* Berkeley/Los Angeles: University of California Press, 1982, Preface.

[4]   Eisler, Riane. *The Chalice and the Blade: Our History, Our Future.* San Francisco: HarperCollins, 1987, 105.

[5]   Sjoo, Monica and Barbara Mor. *The Great Cosmic Mother: Rediscovering the Religion of the Earth.* San Francisco: HarperCollins, 1987, 235.

[6]   Stone, Merlin. *When God Was A Woman.* New York: Harcourt Brace Jovanovich, 1978.

[7]   Starhawk. *The Spiral Dance.* San Francisco: Harper & Row, 1989, 20.

[8]   Gibbs, Nancy and Jeanne McDowell. "How to Revive a Revolution." *Time,* March 9, 1992, 57.

[9]   Dowling, Collette. *The Cinderella Complex.* New York: Simon and Schuster, 1981, 12.

[10]   The Boston Women's Health Book Collective. *The New Bodies Ourselves,* New York: Simon & Schuster, 1992.

[11]   Bowe, Claudia. "Women and Depression: Are We Being Overdosed?" *Redbook,* March 1992, 42.

[12]   De Laszlo, V.S., ed. *The Basic Writings of C.G. Jung.* New York: Random House, 1990, 304.

[13]   Zia, Helen. "Women In Hate Groups." *Ms. Magazine,* March/April 1991, 21.

[14]   Hill, Anita. "The Nature of the Beast." *Ms. Magazine,* January/February 1992, 32.

[15]   *Guide to Bali.* Singapore: Apa Productions Ltd., 1976, 61.

[16] Mead, Margaret. *Man and Female: A Study of the Sexes in a Changing World.* New York: William Morrow and Co., Ltd., 1949, 122.

[17] Plato. *The Republic.* Translated by B. Jowett, M.A. New York: The Modern Library, Random House, 1968, 254.

[18] *Ibid.,* 261.

3

Are You Ready?

We all have a wild woman within. The question is how involved is she in our day-to-day living? If we no longer know who we are, or what we really want for ourselves, then our wild woman is too well hidden. Suppression has kept us from knowing her, and from knowing ourselves. We have learned that if we hold back, then no one can humiliate or attack us. We can no longer be hurt if we build a wall around our hearts (we think), yet we suffer even more due to this separation from life. This wall may dull the pain, but it also keeps away anything really interesting or meaningful. The more connected you are with your wild woman, the more attuned you are to the life force. You can face that wild side that no longer wants to hold back, that wants to break loose of old ways.

The wild woman within is a part of us, and we can choose to call upon her wisdom and energy. For some women this can mean slowly integrating natural, uncensored thoughts and actions into their lives. For others, it may mean a total identity change. I've seen women quit their jobs, leave their partners, dye their hair or begin an entirely new lifestyle. Some women feel they have been waiting forever to break loose so, with this new awareness of their wild sides, they take off in a radical new direction.

The illusion of the completely healed person is obsolete. We do not have to be at a certain point in our healing process, or lives, in order to express our wild woman. It may be easier for us to do if we know more about ourselves; we can be more comfortable being uninhibited if we carry less shame or humiliation in our hearts and no longer criticize ourselves for taking risks.

The following sections are specifically attuned to the emergence of the wild woman. These sections are written to synthesize what women may face as they look more deeply at their wild side. When I first spoke to women about their wild woman they said, "Oh, I'm not wild, I could never do *that*. I'm too frightened or angry. It could change my whole life if I openly expressed my unexposed feelings." Many of these statements stem from fear, shame, internal oppressors or suppression from the outside.

The following topics highlight what some friends and clients have addressed and transformed in their journey toward freedom. These are meant to be suggestions, thoughts to reflect upon. This chapter is meant to leave you with more acceptance of yourself. If you feel a topic does not apply to you, please move on to the next.

My Passage

I had lost my faith. After years of writing and teaching about spirituality, it felt as if mine had evaporated. I'd been in therapy for several years, looking at my childhood issues. I was also working with clients, many with childhood horror stories, and the media was deluged with reports of child abuse. I thought, "What kind of God would allow such crimes in the world? God hasn't done his job right, he hadn't been there for me." According to author Alice Miller, he certainly wasn't there for many other people as well.

When I gave birth to my little girl, Lily, everything that was hidden in my subconscious chose to surface. I would wake up terrified at night. At first I started awakening my husband, or phoning loyal friends in the middle of the night. Then I decided to let them sleep. I would climb three flights of stairs, scream my anguish into pillows, pound my fists on the floor and couches, and kick and flail my arms and legs into the silent night air. It felt as if I were fighting off some dragon I could feel, but not see or confront. I looked for a book titled *Women Who Go Mad After Childbirth*, but I found none. The patriarchal doctors I saw tried to pat my angry hands and tell me I was experiencing some kind of postpartum reaction and it would pass. I knew my pain was being dismissed, and that I was experiencing something more profound than what they said it was. All I could see was the pain in the world. All I could feel was my own fear, anger and depression.

My therapist reminded me that when women have children, their own childhoods become clearer. Was that what was happening to me? I was fortunate to get wonderful support, from both my husband and Lily's godmother, Cathryn, so my baby could get her needs met. But they too were beginning to fear for me. My husband had been feeling the pressure of new parenthood, and living with this terrified woman, for nearly a year. After spending thousands of dollars going to acupressurists, hypnotherapists, herbalists, my homeopath and therapist, this nightmare finally passed.

I was granted a reprieve. Then, when we moved to a house up north away from my long-term friends, I was alone much of the time. Though I didn't remember feeling lonely in my past, I felt it then. We were commuting to the Bay Area: me, seeing clients every other week; my husband, coming home only on the weekends. I tried to write, but I was either busy playing with Lily or she and I were sick all the time. Since I'm a desert person, my system wasn't used to the northern coast. That first summer the town I live in had seven days of sun.

Lily turned two, which turned out to be significant. When I was a little more than two years old, my father, who had a mental illness, told me horror stories of his childhood. He told me how he'd been left to die in his crib by his mother. The neighbors reported a screaming baby to the police, and he was found covered in sores and was hospitalized for a year and a half before being taken to an orphanage. His mother apparently never signed papers allowing him to be adopted, so he was shipped from foster home to foster home. He told me *detailed* stories about how he was beaten, locked in closets, and forced to work to pay for his keep. Since I've rarely experienced a sense of safety in the world, I imagine that I wanted to cry for him, wanted the stories to go away. I probably figured that if they could do those things to the man I loved the most, my father, then things like that could happen to me too.

So, as I found myself an adult, alone, with my two-year-old daughter, these stories began to haunt every part of my being. They were behind every door in our house, reflected back to me in every mirror, every window. I feared that these horrible things were happening to children inside of every house. I was living inside a Stephen King novel, and I couldn't get out. The panic and anxiety were back. That did it. I was convinced there was no benevolence or this wouldn't have happened to people I love, I wouldn't have had to listen to it, and I wouldn't be reliving it today.

One day I was sitting with a male client and he told me something so brutal that had happened to him that I thought I'd have to leave the room. Instead, after he left, I had a panic attack, went to the hospital and told them I was dying. I guess that's how I felt as a kid listening to this stuff, and here I was: a therapist reliving my past.

My pain grew and so did my lack of faith. As Sam Keene, author of *Fire In The Belly*, says, it is possible to become hypnotized by the ugliness in the world. That is what had happened to me. I knew that it was essential for me to find hope and beauty again. Shortly after this realization I left for the desert. My instincts guided me back to a mother mountain I had been visiting for years. I felt, perhaps, that I could leave my stories behind me in my beloved desert. I also knew in order to do this I would finally have to slow down long enough to grieve. As I write later in this chapter, grief is like the transition stage in childbirth: you wonder if you'll ever get through it, and then birth or rebirth follows.

I was alone for the first time in months as I drove across the empty desert. I felt the despair welling up in me. Finally, I was quiet. I could feel what I had worked so hard at pushing away. Feelings of hopelessness, abandonment and rage were right there with me. I could avoid them no longer. I thought I couldn't take any more of it, but some voice inside kept telling me to hang in there, see it through, there was another side.

When I got to my place in the desert I just sat for days and stared at the surrounding mountains. I was definitely in the grieving process — grieving for my past and my uncertain future. The tears hadn't come, which seemed to be holding the other feelings in like a dam. Finally, I forced myself to go to the grocery store. While at the store I saw a mother hit her child. The little girl said, "Ma, don't hit me, I'll be good." I could see the rage in this woman's face. I also saw red, and I began following this woman around the supermarket while she was threatening this child with more abuse.

I had visions of strangling this woman. I tried to walk out of the store but I couldn't. Finally, I said to her, "Excuse me, I saw you hit your child. I'm sure you were hit as a child and it didn't help then, and it won't help now, to hit your child. There's free counseling in town." Her mouth dropped open during my speech, and when I turned around to leave she just went, "Humph." I may not have affected her, but I was certainly stirred up.

When I left I was shaking all over, and the tears started and wouldn't stop. I sat in my car and cried and cried. Here I was in this town, alone, with years of tears that had finally begun to flow. Then I remembered there was a detox center, so I went in there sobbing and asked if someone would talk to me. The receptionist immediately found a beautiful woman, Berjé, who listened and listened. She also talked and her words soothed my pain. She said I couldn't, and didn't have to, save the children of the world. She told me I needed to cry for me, and my pain, for as long as it would take.

As I left her office, I looked up at the mountain and I heard it say to me, "You'll intervene three times in situations with children while you're here." My response was a firm, "No, thank you. I'm here to deal with myself and I'm not going to get involved with other people's problems."

Well, the next day I went to the laundromat — *big mistake!* I heard this child screaming and I tried to turn the other way. Nobody else seemed to hear the cries, so why should I? Finally, I couldn't stop myself. I walked over to where the screaming was coming from and saw an extraordinarily beautiful woman with flaming red hair and blue eyes. She had ten loads of laundry, an infant and a two year old who was crying. She was beginning to lose it.

I walked up to her and said, "I'm a mom, too. Can I help?" She looked completely grateful. She needed help carrying her laundry out to the car, so I did that while entertaining the little boy. She said they hadn't eaten all day, and it had been a long one. We talked about children and then she left. I kept wishing someone from a magazine or film company would discover her, so that she and her kids could eat more and she could have that washing machine she wanted. Again, I cried. I cried for her, I cried for me. Great trip, huh?

After that I decided to stay inside my place and not go outside, that way I could stay out of other people's business. The next day I was lying on my bed, minding my own business, when suddenly two girls — one the fourteen-year-old daughter of the family I was renting from — started sneaking around my place. Then I saw that they were carrying bags that looked suspiciously like runaway gear. The first night I'd met the family, they had told me that Julie had been planning to run away to L.A., but that had all been handled. This was the weekend of the Rodney King uprising and rioting in L.A., so I quickly ran into the kitchen looking for Beth, Julie's stepmother. But she wasn't there. I came outside as she was driving off, already on the chase. I told Beth in what direction the girls were moving and she was able to head them off at the pass. They're all in counseling now. So far, so good.

They were safe, but I had had it! My grief was pouring out all over the place. I decided to go to the mountain for some solace. I had to cross a wide river and do some climbing, and found a place to flatten myself against the earth. I spread my arms and legs out, face down, and just handed myself over to the mountain. I let the earth absorb the pain, and I knew that my three challenges were over, at least for now. The mountain took all I had to give, and in return filled me with strength.

After that, things lightened up quite a bit. I played. I spent time at a pajama party with women friends. We did a "Shedding of the Unwild Skin" (explained in Chapter 4) under an open tepee, and I spent time visiting the hot springs nearby. One adventure seemed to simply follow the next. One day, a man of the Lakota tradition came to my door and said, "If you want to go white-water rafting, be ready in two minutes." I thought, *that* was a direct invitation. I was dressed and out the door in a flash. I can still remember my hysterical laughter as we flew over the rapids (of course, since it was my first rafting trip, I was too ignorant to have any fear).

At some point, it became clear to me that it was time to do something symbolic around letting go of the stories I had been carrying around for years. I decided to go to a person I think of as a medicine woman and ask her to listen to my stories. She agreed. I drew pictures of my past, my father's, and other people's images I had in my head and heart. I told her about them and explained that I was heading to the mountain now to burn the pictures and bury the ashes. She seemed to want to interrupt me regarding burying them, but decided to leave the ceremony to me.

I drove to the place in the river where I had crossed before and saw people there, so I moved on. I found another crossing, but it appeared deeper and more rapid. I hadn't taken into consideration that the snow had melted quickly since I was last there. Nonetheless, I was determined to cross and bury my ashes on *that* side of the mountain, no matter what. I burned my past, waited until the ashes cooled and put them in a bag.

I stepped into the ice-cold water and was immediately swept away. I was bouncing off boulders and fighting for a place to hang on. I knew it was a long and deathly ride to the Rio Grande. I saw a log ahead and turned to grab it to pull myself up; instead I got pulled under. I tried to keep my head above water, but it was a losing battle. I knew I was drowning. Even as I write this I can see the water running over my head. Strange. I didn't think about it until now, but was I looking down on myself?

Suddenly the force of the water set me free. It pushed me through and I hung onto the log, slowly working my way over to a sandy bank in the middle of the river. From there, I climbed over a thin tree branch to safety. The first person I thought of

was my daughter, Lily. Then I realized the river had claimed
my ashes, my past and nearly me.

Fortunately, when I got to the car, I had a change of
clothes because I had been invited to dinner at a friend's house.
I rapidly took off my ice-cold clothing and put on the dry
clothes, turned the heater on and drove off. My friends fed me,
put warm socks on my feet and gave me hot tea. One of them
looked at me and said it might take a while to make sense of all
of this. I didn't know what he was talking about. I was in
shock.

The next day I sat outside my place staring at the mountains and I began to sob. I thought, "I know a lot of people who
would have really missed me if I had died, but would I have
missed my life?" I had lived my childhood, then spent years
denying feelings through my addictions. And now I had spent
years recovering from my addictions and my past. I was sick of
it all, yet I knew that I had nearly died trying to get rid of the
past. I knew that something had happened to me to shake me
up and I had been spared. My psychic friend, Joni McConnell,
called from Seattle and left a message saying, "I'm glad you're
still here."

I sat again, staring at the mountains, and I began to pray.
I knew that if I couldn't find a benevolent power, I was done
for. Just then, Beth called and invited me next door for dinner.
Four men from the Lummi Indian tribe were coming also. Two
of them were diagnosed as terminally ill, and had been told to
leave their land north of Seattle and journey to the hot springs
in the nearby desert.

That evening we sat in a circle around a fire as we ate
dinner. Before we started eating, the leader of the group, Kenny,
sang a song of gratitude for the food we would eat. After
dinner, Kenny spoke of the heart. The Lummi call the heart the
third ear. They hear with the heart; it guides them. I could feel
his faith. Then he drummed and sang a song that I later found
out was the only time he had sung this song outside his tribe.
He had felt so grateful to the springs for the healing he knew
they had received there. Shortly after, it was time for them to
leave. I could see the toll it had taken on their bodies to spend

as much time as they had with us. I felt grateful for my time with them.

As I talked to friends about my near-death experience, I realized I was on a journey to find my wild woman, that part of me who knew who she was and what she wanted in life. That part of me that would have missed life had I died. I had forgotten her under the burdens of everyday life and those of my past. I had been suffering from a lack of faith in myself or any kind of spiritual force. Yet, the mountain had spared me.

I reflected, as I spent time with Native American people, on how much faith they had. They had lived through the Native American holocaust, their land and children had been taken from them, they had suffered slavery and massacres, and many still had their faith. For at least fifteen years, I had seen Anglos turn to the Native American for answers to what was happening on the earth and in their hearts. This had been a controversial issue among pueblo and tribal members. Those who were sharing their knowledge had to strongly debate with other tribal members in order to do so. Many Native Americans still felt there was no reason for them to give information to people who had committed such crimes against them. Yet, more and more, people were teaching those who came, with open hearts, to learn.

Shortly after the evening with the Lummi I was invited to a Sun Dance by a beautiful Native American woman. This year Hopis, Lakotas, Anglos and Aztecs would be dancing. A Lakota man led the ceremony, and the singers and drummers were also Lakota. As part of the ceremony, the dancers fasted for four days. They sat in sweat lodges at night, and danced three to six rounds a day of about two hours each.

Before the four-day dance began, those who would participate went to the high mountains and brought back an aspen tree which they planted in the center of a large circle. They decorated it with colored ribbons. During the ceremony, people were invited to dance outside the circle in support of those within. I danced. Some days they danced under the blazing sun; other days clouds covered the sky. Once, when it began to rain, several tribal members went over to the tree and prayed, and the rain stopped.

When they danced the round, which calls in the wolves, I was allowed to join the pipe ceremony at the end. Four dancers greeted the four of us, and passed the pipe to us three times. The fourth time we were to take the tobacco-filled pipe and keep it smoking by passing it to others in the group. Then we offered the pipe back to the dancers three times. On the fourth they took their pipes, and then full-blooded wolves were brought out by their owner. I thought that wolves must be one of the most beautiful animals alive.

I was not prepared for the skin-piercing that would take place on the third and fourth days. The men offer their flesh because that is what they feel they have to offer the Great Spirit, while women create the miracle of birth. Even though I had been dancing each round, when I realized what was going to happen I turned to leave. Before I could even move my feet, a powerful woman turned to me and said, "Get out of your mind and into your heart. They need your support." I continued dancing as I wept. I had forgotten what a strong heart I had.

Surgical knives had been purchased, and the Lakota leader made four openings — two on each side of the man's chest. He then inserted the bones or sticks that man had made through the skin. Ropes were tied to both ends of the stick and the men would pray to the tree and to the Great Spirit until they were ready to pull back on the ropes, hard enough to break their skin. Sometimes men are hung from the tree to break the skin. I was helped by knowing that these men chose this, and all of them were in a highly spiritual state, not of this world, as they performed this painful offering to the Great Spirit. When their flesh broke, the group would rejoice.

I'll never forget the Aztec dancer, Lonand, who had brought his family and Aztec dancers from Mexico as support for his Sun Dance. Lonand is a beautiful man with dark black hair that falls over his broad shoulders and down his back. His Aztec friends were dressed in jeweled headdress with feathers three feet long and jeweled body shields. They had painted yellow circles around their eyes. They all stood in support of their friend as he chose to do a back-piercing, which can sometimes cause tearing of the muscles. The openings were cut into the skin, near his shoulder blades. In order to break the skin he would need to drag four skulls of bulls around the circle.

He held an eight-foot-long staff in his hand as he dragged the skulls once, twice, three times around the circle, but the skin had not broken. With all his strength he ran around the circle a fourth time. Still the skin had not broken. The leader asked that four children from his family be brought over so they could be seated on the skulls to add weight. What will remain with me forever is the look of faith in that man's eyes as he held his staff up to the Great Spirit, and began to drag his heavy burden until his flesh broke. Free at last, he ran around the circle in celebration.

I hugged each dancer before returning home. I was exhausted. I thought of their faith, their commitment to the earth, to spirit. I thought of my growing faith in the mountain, in the sagebrush and the dirt outside my window, and a benevolent spirit that had spared my life.

That night I dreamt that a cross between Yoda (from the movie *Star Wars*) and Elizabeth Kübler-Ross came to me. They told me to get on with my purpose, that I'd been wallowing in the past too long. I was used to Elizabeth talking to me that way — straightforward, you might say. I asked about my purpose, but woke up before I got an answer — just like the two of them to do something like that.

I went once again to the mountain, this time walking up and around before lying down. I listened to her, and to my own heart. I heard, "It's time to go home now — to be part of a family and to stop holding back what you know." I wasn't really comfortable with what I heard. The word "family" had always frightened me. I didn't know how to be close, only to move away. I also felt, deep down, that Lily was probably better off with other people than with me, because I had too many feelings and I was afraid she'd be burdened by them. Even though people had told me I was a good mother, I had felt there was something wrong with me. As for the writing, I knew exactly what the mountain was telling me. It was time to stop being so nice. I'd spent years being nice, in an effort not to offend people. It was time to let that go. I could feel this growing strength inside that cared less and less about what people thought of me and my writing. In fact, I had recently noticed how often I was speaking my mind and doing outrageous things, no matter how others reacted.

I knew I wanted to leave for home soon, yet I had already made plans to go to Denver. As I drove to Denver, I had time to think more about the changes that were happening inside me, and how these could be reflected in my day-to-day life. While visiting my close friend, Anne, my left foot started hurting. I told her that my foot hurt only when something was going on with my father. Then I remembered, "Oh my God, my father lives in Denver!" I didn't hesitate; I called him and we met. He had continued to heal and change as the years had gone by. He said to me, "I know you're angry at me. Will you tell me why?" I told him, "Those stories you told me when I was two years old — I feel like you stole my innocence." He listened through my tears and responded, "I am so sorry, I didn't know any better. I read books now, I know what I did was wrong. I'm sorry if I hurt you."

We talked about many things. One thing I found remarkable was that I had never thought highly of the word "forgiveness," nor had he. When he was growing up he had hated his mother, who had left him, and some of the cruel foster parents who had followed. He had held onto that hatred for seventy years. Then something had happened to him: a year or so ago, he simply became willing to forgive them. Simultaneously his blood pressure dropped, and he went off all medication. During this visit I could feel that I had given up my need to carry his stories, that my father was O.K. now, and that it was no longer my job to carry someone else's pain.

I returned to the desert town for a few days and reflected on the faith that was slowly creeping back into my life. It was a new kind of faith for me — faith in the earth, the sagebrush, the mountain. In listening to the beat of my own heart. I felt lighter. I could tell that I felt less controlling and more willing to live in the moment.

Getting to know my wild woman has added a new aspect to my personality. I fear death less, and I am more willing to take risks with people and situations. I often feel uninhibited — not worrying about what others are thinking of me. I say yes more often, and my sense of humor has returned. I'm less serious. It's as if I know everything will work out and if the bumpy times come, I will live through them.

Slow Down, You Move Too Fast

If you stay still long enough, you are going to feel your feelings. Depending on what is going on in your life, this can be a comfortable, or a lousy, experience.

When I look around, it appears that many people are trying to outrun their feelings. People are moving faster and faster with no time to live in the moment — we have espresso cafes, the Japanese have oxygen bars. This running around can come from societal pressures, women working full- or part-time jobs, and taking care of or being the sole supporter of their families. There are also many distractions: movies, plays, concerts, galleries. For many there is an addiction to movement. If I move fast enough I won't have to feel what is underneath, I won't have to know who I am.

It takes time for that inward journey, to uncover our wild woman. We need to slow down to feel her and welcome her in. Like getting to know anyone, we need to slow down long enough to see them, give them the time they deserve so we can know one another. It also means discarding what our parents and society have always wanted of us, and discovering what we want for ourselves; what is wild, natural, creative, sensual, perhaps uncontrollable, angry and irresponsible at times.

Finding ways to slow down can appear to be a monumental task for many women, yet it is possible. Each woman will find her own way. I've found going away to the mountains, to a small rural area, an automatic way to slow down. I also find it very unsettling at times. I think, "Oh no, what will I do there?" For women who do not want to leave their area, who cannot afford the time or expense, there are many options.

There are daily behaviors we can incorporate into our lives that will slow us down. There can be some time in the day when you stop everything and sit in a chair or lie down, even if it's only for five minutes. Maybe you'll want to sit outside, examine people's faces as they go by, or notice the cloud formations — simply do nothing and let your mind wander. Baths with candlelight and herbs are wonderful for nurturing the body. Some women find it calming and vital to get up early in the morning to meditate and reflect before beginning their day. Any time of day can be a good time for this. I like to take time, wherever I am, to notice what the sky looks like, to absorb the ground beneath my feet, whether it's concrete or earth.

Walking is also good for slowing down. Lying flat on the floor, or earth, and feeling the vibrations can bring us into the moment. The trick is getting the mind to take a vacation so you can enjoy the present time. I noticed, while spending time with indigenous cultures, that they move so that they can hear the wind, feel the earth, be alert to what is happening around them, sense people's spirits, intuitively know what is happening with one another. This is the power of living in the present. Less becomes more, and what is artificial becomes more obvious.

Watching the people of the Tiwa pueblo has been a learning experience for me. For years, I've gone to their corn dances on a regular basis. They tell visitors that the dance will start around one o'clock, but the elders do not carry a watch and sometimes it's three or four o'clock before the dance begins. At first I was like the other tourists, irritated that things weren't happening on *my* time schedule. Some people leave, others grumble. It usually rains, so people head for their cars. When I'd look up at the four-story pueblo walls, I'd see the elders wrapped in white and blue sheets. They'd appear to be observing and feeling everything around them — the sky, the mountain, the moisture in the air.

Finally, when they agree it is time, the corn dance begins. I always experience a swell of emotion as I watch this ceremony. Now, after years of experience, I come with a poncho and a jug of water. I spend time looking at the mountain and watching the elders at their work. Do these men, wrapped in sheets, standing upon ancient pueblo walls, know what they do for my soul?

Another example of the contrast between the fast and the slow was when I met a friend of mine for a counseling session that was of great personal and business importance to both of us. I had just returned from the quiet world of the desert, slowed down and not yet prepared for the Bay Area, let alone this meeting. We had made an appointment with a negotiator months ago, so I knew I needed to show up. My friend entered the room with that fast-moving efficient energy, probably having had a cappuccino or two. I was moving, *maybe*, as fast as a turtle. She said she'd been preparing three and a half weeks for this meeting, so she opened the discussion.

As hard as I tried, I couldn't understand a word she was saying. All I knew was that I was feeling sad and angry and she was feeling frightened, but I didn't know of what. We tried to get to specifics, but my brain was apparently short-circuited. The negotiator kept interrupting my friend to ask me what I thought. I told her I felt angry and distant. My brain was having trouble catching up with my brilliant and fast-talking friend. Finally, after two and a half hours of listening to her talk, she started crying and said, "I feel that you don't love me anymore." I heard that. It was as if the sun and the moon had entered the room. I went to her and held her, and told her that everything would be O.K.

I'm not trying to say that moving fast is wrong and moving like a turtle is right. It's simply that what happened with my friend is an example of what can happen when we slow down. Our feelings become more present to us in the moment.

In *The Sun My Heart*, Thich Nhat Hahn writes, "Each thought, each action in the sunlight of awareness becomes sacred. In this light, no boundary exists between the sacred and the profane. I must confess it takes me a bit longer to do the dishes, but I live fully in every moment, and I am happy. Washing the dishes is at the same time a means and an end. That is, not only do we do the dishes in order to have clean dishes, we also do the dishes just to do the dishes, to live fully in each moment while washing them.

"If I am incapable of washing dishes joyfully, if I want to finish them quickly so I can go and have a cup of tea, I will be equally incapable of drinking the tea joyfully. With the cup in my hands I will be thinking about what to do next, and the fragrance and the flavor of the tea, together with the pleasure of drinking it, will be lost. I will always be dragged into the future, never able to live in the present moment."[1]

The more one practices slowing down, the more natural it becomes. Laura Davis, co-author of *The Courage to Heal*, says, "Now when people ask me how far along they are in the healing process (of incest), I ask them how well they are taking care of themselves? To me, how people nurture themselves and pace themselves is a real indicator of this."[2]

We can slow down, so we can feel the beat of our wild hearts, and allow that beat to grow louder and stronger, listen for its wisdom. Some people associate this beat with that of the natives, for example, the tribal groups in the Amazon or the beat of the Native American drum. Listening can bring us into the present moment. If we are in the moment, we will be able to feel what is needed for us to know. Our feelings will not be shoved into the shadow, and our wild woman will be free to guide us.

Slowing down and allowing our feelings to enter our lives is perhaps one of the most difficult things for people to do in our culture. This is because slowing down is not just watching television all day (although escapism can be therapeutic at times); it is letting yourself stop, notice, feel, listen. It's a strange concept for Westerners and does not have to be done full time. You may want to start with stopping and listening five or ten minutes a day. You're sure to hear or notice something you may have otherwise missed — a bug, an interesting face, a creative idea or a feeling.

Addictions

Our true wild side can remain hidden from us through our addictions. Just as moving too fast can be an addiction, so can anything else. As Anne Wilson Schaef believes, we live in an addictive society; don't experience your pain, don't let your feelings interfere with your life and your desire to stay happy.

As a society, we appear to be afraid of feelings, so we can always find some form of addiction to keep our feelings from us: drugs and alcohol, overworking, compulsive shopping, excessive hours spent watching television — anything that will keep our unconscious suppressed. Many fear that their feelings may be overwhelming, or get in the way of their being productive. If we listened attentively to our feelings, they might challenge our current lifestyles.

We learn quickly in childhood not to trust our feelings. Trust can be broken in many ways; perhaps a lie, such as the child who hears her parents screaming at each other and then is told that "We're not angry." Or a child says, "I'm scared," and the parents say, "No you're not, there's nothing to be scared of." Trust in one's feelings soon goes out the door. Children need to feel they can trust a parent and that the parent will be there for them. As a result of this innate need, a child will almost always choose to trust the adult's feedback rather than her or his own experience.

Distrusting our feelings eventually leads to inner conflict. This conflict leads to tension that eventually needs to be released. For some people this tension is released through engaging in addictive behavior. One of the first addictions for a child becomes the search for a way to maintain control. They ask themselves, "How can I make things more manageable? How can I make these mixed-up feelings go away?" Children seek control by keeping their rooms compulsively clean, by throwing a tantrum in order to be the center of attention, by taking care of mom and dad, by cooking for them or listening to their problems in an effort to make their parents' lives happier.

Addictive behavior either changes form, or we add layers of addiction to core addictions as we move into adulthood. For example, a person who was a caretaker in childhood is still a caretaker, and in adulthood may expand to become a workaholic, shopaholic, alcoholic or self-abuser. Everything gets projected outside of ourselves. Our addictions, rather than our feelings, become what is important to us. Meanwhile, the wild woman inside remains increasingly in the shadows.

Some people believe their wild woman comes alive when they are in the middle of active addiction: chemical use, over-spending, sexual addiction. That's the wild addict that becomes activated which has some of the qualities of the wild woman — energy, spontaneity, uncensored action. Yet, this is not the true wild woman. In fact, addictions are destructive because they keep us from hearing our heart and getting to know the natural, spontaneous wild woman that is a powerful force in our lives. The true wild woman carries an energy that continues and grows, not an energy that leads to self-destruction and avoidance of the truth.

Philip Kavanaugh, M.D., author of *Magnificent Addiction*, writes, "Addiction is much more than simply being hooked on substances or behaviors. I consider several words to be synonymous with addiction and sometimes use them interchangeably; compulsion, crazy, enslavement, obsession. We seem desperate for control. Knowledge, possessions, recognition, perfect health, meaningful relationships. It is more than a need. It is an unhealthy addiction, one that lies at the root of all other unhealthy addictions. In fact, I call our compulsive drive to be in control the Master Addiction."[3]

The problem is what to do about this. Since addiction, in one form or another, has been a way of life for many, how do we begin to uncover the layers? Is it really worth it? Do we really want to let go of control and experience a life where we have to feel and eventually trust a power within and around us?

This is an individual choice. Usually what happens is that someone hits bottom (can no longer stand their life and where their addiction has taken them) so they seek help through a treatment and/or an anonymous program, such as alcoholics, overworkers or overeaters anonymous. As they begin their recovery from an addiction, feelings they haven't felt in years begin to surface. Most people seek counseling at this point, in order to understand what is happening to them. In time they become aware of more and more addictive behavior. I had one client who said, "I can't breathe without being addictive."

That's why I have always liked what the founders of Alcoholics Anonymous wrote: " . . . the primary purpose of this program is to find a power greater than ourselves."[4] As long as we are hanging onto any form of addiction or control, it's difficult for a force within or without us to do its job in our lives.

Recovery from addiction takes time. There's generally a period of at least one year where people go through a grieving process. First, they deny that their problem was as severe as it really was. Then, as they begin to accept the truth about their addiction, they feel anger, depression, and despair at the loss of a "friend" (their addiction) that they have relied on to keep them from the pain inside. As each addiction is dealt with, all the way through to the initial addiction around the desperate desire for control, the grieving process is repeated. This, too, takes time. A sign of an obsessive personality is the need to rid oneself of every addiction all at once. That can become simply another addiction.

Of course, if an addiction is causing an immediate life-or-death situation, then an intervention is, hopefully, made by a Higher Power, another person (possibly the police) or a treatment program.

Samantha came to see me for a life-threatening drinking problem. She had already been arrested once for Driving Under the Influence (DUI), and she was having trouble staying sober longer than eight weeks at a time. Besides working with me, I encouraged her to go to a support group for people dealing with the same problem. Since she said she hated Alcoholics Anonymous, I referred her to a group led by a facilitator. She attended this group in addition to the DUI group the court had mandated. With the support she received from her Higher Power, counseling, and two groups a week, she made it past the first eight weeks, then a ninth week, and so on. Her self-esteem lifted and she felt some hope for her life.

Later, she was ready and able to deal with her other life-threatening problems, smoking and overeating. She gradually became more aware of her feelings, which was not easy for her. Her addictions had been her "friends" in that they had numbed the pain from her past. However, as she saw her way through the past into the present, there was less of a need for the layers of addiction she had used to coat her true self. We need to have compassion for ourselves and others as the layers of addiction begin to peel away and our true selves are exposed.

As the layers lift, we can become more familiar with the wild woman. She can be part of your program of recovery. If you listen to her, you will hear the truth and feel what is real.

Bobby was working on her shopping addiction — her attempt to meet her inner needs by looking outside herself and compulsively accumulating beautiful material things. Though she had plenty of money, she could never buy enough to fill up the empty space she had inside.

During a session, I asked her to close her eyes and see if she could invite in an image of her wild woman. She knew immediately that the woman before her was her wild woman, but she wasn't what Bobby had expected or approved of. Her wild woman was wearing a straw hat and had her bare hands buried in the earth she was tending. Bobby wondered what this woman could possibly have to offer her? She watched her for a while, and observed how at peace she seemed to be as she worked in the garden.

Then the woman turned her attention to Bobby, and it was as if she saw right through to Bobby's soul. She asked, "What can I do for you?" Since Bobby felt so desperate, I encouraged her to converse with this straw-hatted woman. Bobby said, "I don't know any way to fill this great emptiness inside of myself. Please help me." Her wild woman turned and looked at her for quite a while, then answered, "What do you really want that hole filled with?" as she pointed her mud-covered fingers toward Bobby's stomach. Bobby immediately began to cry, and told her that she wanted her father to love and approve of her, but he never had. Her wild woman continued to hold her hand out toward her stomach and told Bobby to imagine that her whole being was completely filled with that kind of love. Bobby did this and was able to feel the force of her wild woman supporting her.

Bobby began to feel the beat of her own vibrancy. This was the beginning of an ongoing relationship with her wild woman. Besides continuing in counseling to work on her issues concerning her father, Bobby was able, due in part to the strength and support she got from her wild woman, to join a group for people working on releasing compulsive spending from their lives. In this group she made new friends and expanded her network of support. Over time, she felt less of a need to fill her emptiness the old, addictive way. To the amazement of many of her friends, she even took up gardening and found herself enjoying more time out of doors.

When addiction is no longer hiding from us that natural, spontaneous, spirited part of ourselves, we can feel more and trust the wisdom we hear from within. As one becomes fulfilled, the fear of living changes. One welcomes life and has no need to hide from it.

Our Healthy Conscience

The healthy conscience is the part of us that is nonjudgmental and wise. It oversees our actions, insuring that we are out of danger and not self-destructive. Our healthy conscience supports our desires, nurtures us, and often puts a voice to our gut feelings. It is not our intuition or inner guidance, but part of its job is to listen to our intuition and pass on the knowledge. We can develop a part of our mind that is encouraging, alert and protective, by retraining how we think. Left on its own, our mind will rattle off all kinds of nonsense. Think of what it has gathered from your family, peers, the media. For example, I heard a man speak who described his inner voice as a vulture that perched above his bedpost. When he would awaken in the morning, it would begin with such comments as, "Hey, you haven't gotten nearly enough sleep, you'll be tired all day. Do you feel that numbness in your left arm? It might be a heart attack. Better call 911. Look at the weather outside, too sunny, this is going to be a foul day." By the time this man finished listening to his negative voice, he barely had the energy to get out of bed.

The alternative to this self-abuse is to build a strong, healthy conscience that when we wake says something like,

"Well, you're awake, good for you. Yes, it's a work day, but think of that exciting research and writing you're doing. You may be able to track down that guy you've been looking for the last week. If you get up now and get some tea, you might even get a moment to yourself." The healthy conscience can get us out of bed, encourage us in our work, our love life, our creativity.

There's no limit to how we can retrain our mind to be on our side. Our healthy conscience is the part that truly gives us the option to make our own rules, and find ourselves in situations we never thought we'd get into and still be safe. Our healthy conscience knows the difference between dangerous behavior and what is wild. For example, your conscience knows the difference between having unsafe sex (life-threatening) and jumping out of an airplane with a parachute (scary, but relatively safe, if you know what you are doing).

One day I was standing at the top of a thirty-foot rock staring down at the water below. I wanted to leap through the air to the water. The problem was, I had no idea how deep the water was — two, six, ten feet? However, I was getting ready to jump anyway. But I heard this voice say, "Check the depth of the water." I just wanted to recklessly jump but I had second thoughts, so I climbed down the rock, checked the depth of the water (about ten feet) and made sure there were no rocks down there. Then I climbed back up with a clear conscience. In the long run, it really didn't take any of my fun away. There's something so amazing about living in the present. There I was, thirty feet between me and that pool of water. I thought only of that jump, nothing else in the world mattered. Then I leapt off the rock into the water below. It was glorious.

However, I have to admit that I haven't always listened to my voice of health. Sometimes I jump anyway. This has left me in precarious situations. As wild women, we sometimes walk a thin line between living on the edge and being destructively out of control. That's why we need our healthy conscience. If we listen, we'll receive support and guidance. For example, perhaps you're driving too fast and passing cars swiftly and safely, then you get this feeling to slow down, or an even louder message like, "No." That is the time to listen to your healthy conscience.

It's taken years to learn negative dialogue, so it can take years to undo the damage and begin to listen to a more balanced truth about ourselves. Descartes, after a lifetime of study, assessed that "You are what you think." That was his entire spiritual foundation. Do you want your spiritual foundation to say you're a piece of junk or a beautiful woman?

Begin by noticing how you talk to yourself. Are you abusive and repressive? If so, that can be changed. To develop or strengthen your healthy conscience, you can begin with a voice that encourages you to try new things which will build faith in yourself. For example, going down the slide backwards like the kids do at the park, or getting your hands covered in dirt as you try some gardening, or dancing naked to your favorite music. When that internal oppressor comes in and says, "You look foolish" or "Shouldn't you be doing something other than dancing naked?" you can answer, "No. If I break loose now, I'll feel better the rest of the day."

You know you're dealing with your healthy conscience when you hear messages of support and acceptance. It can take time to develop this part fully. Most people are still learning to heal the critic and allow for more self-acceptance. You can develop a healthy conscience by saying helpful things to yourself. While you're working on a project you can say, "Hey, this is really good work I'm doing." Or when you're tired and your child has pulled at you all day, you can commend yourself by saying, "I got through a rough day without being grumpy with my child."

Our healthy conscience is like a loving mother or tutor that encourages us to move forward and express more of who we are. It can stand strong in the face of the oppressor. It supports our breaking free of oppressive ways of being and thinking. A woman described what it was like to break loose. She'd currently been addressing her incest issues, and she shared that she felt a desperate urge to get out of the cage that she had built around herself. A few days later she did some powerful rage work in an incest group she belonged to. As a result, she said, "I just want to tell everybody to get out of their cages, walk in front of those bars and live!" The wild woman had emerged.

You can create in your mind any form of healthy conscience. For some it's a human, an animal, or perhaps a voice without form. I have several images of people or animals that come to mind at different times. For example, the wise Native American woman that sits by the fire, or writer Lillian Hellman who paces with a cigarette in her mouth saying, "Words, words, words. Say what you mean." (She's probably repeating what Hammett said to her.) One of my strongest images, that I feel has literally saved my life, is that of Billie Holiday. When I was scared, almost too frightened to go on, I would feel her come sit by my bed and sing to me. I'd hear the words, "Them that's got shall get, Them that's not shall lose, So the Bible says, And it still is news. Mama may have, And Papa may have, But God bless the child that's got her own, that's got her own."[5] I needed her soulful love to make it through. Others need fiery Goddesses or wild animals to bring them their wisdom and color. Depending on the situation or day, our healthy conscience can look or sound different to us.

We're so used to listening to the repressive such as, "Don't do that," "Are you crazy?" or "You might fail." However, the more we follow the healing words, the stronger the words will become. Our healthy conscience needs to be strong to supersede the voice of an internal oppressor. There will also be times when you find them doing battle inside your brain. The best thing is to step back and listen to both sides, then decide what really fits your nature. For example, perhaps you are considering asking your employer for a raise. Your oppressor says, "Don't chance it, it could make him see you as too aggressive or greedy, why don't you wait?" Your healthy conscience conflicts with these ideas saying, "You've done great work for this company for nearly a year. The accounts you've brought in have brought them big money. Now's the time." After hearing both sides of the issue, you may choose to do what your oppressor suggests. You may not feel ready for change today, yet one can stay open to change in the future.

As we build our healthy conscience it will feel safe for our wild woman to emerge. She's not going to feel like coming up from the shadows if she's going to be abused, mutilated or burned at the stake. However, if treated with respect, she will increasingly show herself to us.

Our Internal Oppressor

Our "internal oppressor" is the part of our mind that tries to control us. It tells us what we should and should not do. We've all been oppressed in one form or another, so we know what this feels like. An oppressor will use any form of abuse and criticism to get us to do what it wants. Its favorite words are "don't" and "should." For example, it will spout such statements as, "You *should* stay quiet, *don't* ruffle the feathers, *don't* take risks, be cool, be respectable, stay responsible and, most importantly, stay in control." Then, in tandem with your inner critic, you hear such things as, "What a fool you are for dating a guy fifteen years younger than you, why don't you grow up? Be wild? *Don't* do that, that's dangerous. Something could happen to you. You're not a good enough worker or mother. Everything you do is wrong."

Most people adapted the voice of their internal oppressor from the early authority figures in their lives, beginning with their family, their first teachers and society. Either you were directly oppressed as a child and/or you saw those around you being oppressed. Whether or not it is you or someone you love being oppressed it is hard for you, when you're a child, to separate the two. For example, Meg, a child of four, overheard her mother tell her father, "You're crazy, what a stupid idea. How can you trust anything you think?" Later in life, Meg is told frequently by her mother, "You're crazy, like your father." She then adopts the belief that she can't trust what she thinks and feels and, as an adult, continually asks others if her thoughts and decisions are O.K. There are far too many examples of such emotional oppression, including physical and sexual abuse, which leave a child shamed, enraged and definitely repressed.

A friend of mine, who has the most beautiful deep laugh, told me that her father had humiliated her publicly for her laughter. He'd told her in front of her relatives, "You laugh like a donkey." Because of this, she'd tried to hide her laugh and it had come out as a wheeze. When she later realized that her father had been cruel and what he'd said wasn't true, she no longer let her internal voice of control tell her how to laugh. As I listen to her deep laugh, it pains me to think that she felt shame about anything so beautiful.

Even if your messages were not as direct as the examples above, women still learn while growing up what is acceptable and what is not. We learn at home, in the classroom, in the workplace and from the media. We learn how to dress and act so we'll be liked. We learn what to do to achieve what we think we want in life. The main job of the internal oppressor is to keep everything under control. If we just do this or that, everything will be O.K. I'll have security and safety, and no one will hurt me. I'll have a good job, a family, all the things I think I want. The more traumatic the environment you came from, the more you'll want and need to be in control to feel safe. Our internal oppressor says NO to most things that will cause change.

The first step in dealing with the internal oppressor is to identify it. Begin to notice how often you hold yourself back from doing something spontaneous or fun. Begin to listen to what you are saying to yourself. Bring this part of your consciousness out into the open. Then you can make decisions, not take orders, and you will have the power of choice. Do I want to do what this oppressor is demanding, or do I want to try something different? At first it may not feel like you have a choice. You may be so used to taking orders and believing this part of yourself that it will take time to identify and then change what you've been thinking. You may also make the decision to continue taking orders from your oppressor. You may decide that your oppressor has the right idea about how to handle a certain situation — at least for now.

You may hear your oppressor as your mind talking to you, or you may see an image of your oppressor. The clients

I've worked with in hypnosis generally see an image of their internal oppressor. Sarah, who had been a client for several months, experienced many fears in her life and was terrified to follow her creative instincts. While under hypnosis, her internal oppressor appeared and she saw an image of the female prison warden of a concentration camp. The image came from Lina Wertmuller's film, *Seven Beauties*. If there was ever an image of evil, the warden was it. This warden emotionally and physically tortured prisoners just because she could.

With such an image of her oppressor, it took some time for Sarah to begin a dialogue with this frightful part of herself. This warden would spew hideous demands and insults at her, preventing her from trying anything new or possibly risky. Sarah wanted to make a living as a dancer in the music video industry but, of course, her warden would have none of it. Over time she was able to stand up to this domineering woman and begin a conversation. It was helpful that when she began to listen carefully to the voice of her internal oppressor, she realized it was the voice of her parents. She was now able to take the mask off the warden, see her mother and father and inner dialogue with them. She was able to see that she was listening to her parent's beliefs, such as "You can't dance, it's against our religion. It's bad to make too much money. You'll never do anything useful with your life or be successful. It's shameful to dress like that."

Sarah is very creative and, as a child, she would escape the family nightmare by going into her room to create jewelry, paintings, collages, fashion designs and dance. Eventually she was able to sort out the truths from the lies in what her parents had told her, and was able to allow herself to dress the way she wanted, make money as a dancer, be noticed, and work in movies and music videos. She is currently starting her own dance company. These changes happened bit by bit. After so many years of indoctrination, it was not easy to find trust for her desires.

Not everyone's oppressor is so visual to them; some only hear the words or feel the fear in their bodies. It can also come in different forms at different times. Projected outward it could be your boss, your lover, your father. What matters is being aware of your oppressor and knowing what you have allowed to dominate you.

Many women need to discharge the rage they feel toward the oppressor they've lived with. In the above situation, Sarah was able in her imagination to put her parents in a prison camp, have them suffer the abuses she felt they deserved, and then rant and rave about their lies and abuse toward her. She was later able to feel her own loss and grieve for the childhood she deserved but missed. She was eventually able to let go of their ideas and build a healthy conscience within to support her.

People have different means for dealing with their oppressor. After identifying this voice, some people simply tell this part of themselves to shut up and then turn to their healthy conscience for support. Others need to be more violent or physical. I know one woman who made a picture of her oppressor and used it as a dart board. Then she invited others over to do the same. They made pictures of their oppressors or repressive organizations and threw darts at them. It turned into quite a party. This woman was also able, when ready, to talk to her oppressor and negotiate some peaceful solutions to the uncharitable treatment she was receiving from within. Once the anger is released, people are more willing to enter into conversation with this part of themselves as equals, not victims or rebels.

Our rebel is different from our wild woman. The wild woman may enact what appear to be rebellious acts, but not without being aware of what is natural to her. It is common, however, for people's rebels to appear in reaction to the repression they've undergone. For example, the dart board party was a fun way to let that rebellious teenager out. The rebel, like a teenager, just wants to break loose of parental rules and controls. She becomes increasingly aware of the rules she has lived with, and now wants to go in the opposite direction. This is a normal developmental stage that many people were not allowed to express, so later in life they may receive the opportunity to do this in a variety of ways. It's like Maria, who had been holding back her sexuality for years, yet living what she felt was a fairly happy housewife role. This was obviously not all of what she felt, for one night she met an Italian painter and ran off to Rome with him. She left her family and opened up to her sexuality and creativity in a way she hadn't experienced in years.

Even though rebellion can be necessary in many cases, in Maria's situation the wild woman may have thought more about her husband and children's feelings before leaving, instead of after. She may very likely have made the same decision, but prepared her family for what was happening. The rebel just wants to strike out at the oppressor and, like a teenager, often does not think before she leaps. The rebel can also lead us into addictive behaviors which, although fun at first, can later be self-destructive. For example, are we feeling love or sexual addiction? Or are we letting go of restrictive ways of being? In many cases, there's a very fine line between these.

It's times like this when we need to call upon the wisdom of our wild woman and our healthy conscience. Yet our internal oppressor has no need for our healthy conscience. It's simply interested in maintaining control, and Maria's running off to Italy certainly doesn't fit into that category.

For many, the internal oppressor was initially developed to keep us safe in an unsafe world. "If I criticize or control myself first, then they won't be able to do it to me." This gives the child and the adult a larger sense of control which, as a child, was so desperately needed if one lived in an out-of-control environment. Safety becomes control. It takes a spiritual faith in order to begin to let go. It also takes practice. You can begin by saying, "Well, maybe if I keep my hands off this situation, the Higher Power can move in there and come up with a better solution." Then, when positive results occur, you may be willing to try this more often. There are mystics who live their entire lives filled with the thought and feeling of this spiritual force; for them, every day is filled with the miracle of life. As we become more trusting, we can let go and be more uninhibited. As we experience this and begin to follow our hearts rather than our oppressive minds, we will automatically become free of our internal and external oppressors.

Julie wanted to be an actress. Her internal voice told her that she was too old and didn't have any talent. Her husband affirmed all her fears and asked her when would she begin to take her life seriously and make more money. Despite the criticism, she had friends and a healthy conscience that encouraged her to move forward toward her dream. She began taking acting classes, and in her spare time trying out for parts. Her faith in herself grew and her healthy conscience supported her desire to do what she wanted in life. However, she wrestled with this inside and out and had to be true to her faith in her desires. If the oppressor thinks it's losing ground, it will up the ante of insults to get your attention and maintain control. In her case, her husband threatened divorce if she didn't get back to business. That frightened her. Her fear was the oppressor making its last hurrah. Just when you think your internal oppressor is finally quieting down, it comes forward with a barrage of insults and threats. "How can I control this woman?" it screams.

Although Julie was vulnerable to the criticism she was hearing both externally and internally, she continued to pursue her dreams. She began getting acting parts and receiving encouragement from others in the field. She also got a divorce. It was no longer tolerable for her to live with someone who had so little faith in her.

Ninety percent of the work is to identify our internal oppressor and to acknowledge the feelings of shame, fear, rage, despair and grief it has caused. If the oppressor is in control, our wild woman will stay in hiding. But once we identify our oppressor, whether internal or external, and begin to say no to what we don't want and yes to what we do, our wild woman can emerge.

Shame

We've all had feelings of shame. Shame includes feelings of being less than others, worthless, undeserving and, basically, that there is something innately wrong with us.

As wild women, it is particularly important to confront our feelings of shame. I find that the expression of one's wild woman, or even thinking about expressing her, is one of the fastest ways to bring feelings of shame to the surface. A woman risks speaking out in a public meeting and later feels she did something wrong, or her child comes home from school and tells her that some kids made fun of what he was wearing, and she feels deep shame.

Underneath is that voice saying, "I did it wrong. Somebody disapproves of me, and that means I am 'less than.'" Deep beneath that voice are memories of other times we were humiliated by someone, told we were wrong, stupid or bad. For many, this begins in childhood when children are emotionally put down by parents, authority figures and friends. Perhaps as children they felt unwanted or didn't live up to someone's expectations, or they weren't "good enough" to belong to the "right" group; their skin wasn't the "right" color or they were "eggheads." Different in some way. Then, for many, there is the emotional, physical and sexual abuse that a child can only reconcile by believing there is something wrong or bad about them — otherwise this harm, this horror, wouldn't be happening. Laura Davis and Ellen Bass, authors of *The Courage to Heal*, write how the incested child is told that it is her or his fault and the child ends up feeling bad or wrong. They write, "Recognizing that you were not to blame means that the people you loved did not have your best interests at heart."[6]

Author Alice Miller writes that shame forms in our earliest years when we are slighted or ignored. In *The Drama of the Gifted Child*, she describes when she observed parents getting an ice cream for themselves but not for their child. The child kept screaming for a cone, but the parents would give the child a bite and then take it away again. The child sobbed in rage and humiliation for not being understood or treated with respect. Miller also described how the bed-wetting of the famous film maker, Ingmar Bergman, was dealt with by his parents. His parents would make him wear a red dress to school the next day so everyone would know what he had done — as if shaming him would solve the problem.

The list of ways people can be shamed goes on and on. Being humiliated by others, which generally causes a feeling of shame, is a means of control. It keeps us in line by getting people to act, dress and think a certain way. All the information we have collected from our parents, peers, authority figures and the media becomes a part of the internal oppressor's armament. We then begin to shame ourselves: always watching to be sure that we look O.K., talk the "right" lingo, meet the standards of our society.

Betsy, a client, had always wanted to be a healer. Her father was an attorney and had put down her goal as frivolous, and gave her looks that implied that there must be something wrong with her. Betsy, wanting to please her father, became a paralegal and found that she was increasingly miserable. As she worked through her father's repressive voice of criticism, she started feeling better and decided to risk taking classes in body work and hands-on healing. She still felt uncomfortable and wouldn't tell anyone about it, but she pursued her interests with a sense of joy she hadn't felt in a long time. It turned out she had quite a gift for her healing work, and she eventually opened a practice. She and her father still do not discuss what she does for a living, but her daily mantra of "I am not ashamed. I am not bad or wrong" worked for her. Instead of listening to the internal oppressor, Betsy chose to listen to her healthy conscience and follow the instincts of her wild woman.

We can utilize our healthy conscience to undo the harm that was done. Instead of listening to the internal oppressor, we can listen to the voice of sanity that says, "You are not worthless or shameful. You are a worthwhile, creative woman who can choose to live your life as you want. We're no longer victims." We can learn to take care of ourselves. A person or institution can try to humiliate us, but we can refuse to be shamed.

Shame is such a painful feeling that it can take over your entire mood. A simple thing could happen where you felt brushed off, or not listened to, and suddenly this feeling of shame overwhelms you. If you did not suffer from feelings of shame already, you'd find you were either annoyed or didn't notice the slight. If you did notice it, you could take care of it directly. However, for many this is difficult to do. What's happening is you're reenacting an old wound. This is when it's important to see if you can uncover that memory. In this case, it would be wise at some point in the day to ask yourself where that feeling of being "less than" stems from. Ask your wild woman to assist you, then tell whomever that source of shame is, a person or an institution, "You can have all your shame back, I don't deserve to be treated like that. . . ." This will help rid you of the shame at the core. It takes time to heal, but then, one day, you'll notice that you're saying to yourself, "I have no reason to feel shame. I am powerful and worthwhile."

For example, a friend and I were out and she ran into a man she'd met before. She reintroduced herself and me, and said a few words to try and start a conversation. He looked her up and down, snubbed her, got into his BMW and drove away. I was shocked. "What a jerk," I said. "How dare he snub you that way." I was feeling shame for myself and for her. She could not have cared less. "It's his problem," she said, and went on to talk about other things. I thought, what a healthy response. To her it wasn't even worth a verbal retort to the man, or a moment of her time afterward.

A repressive society works through the use of shame. It controls the way people think and act by setting the standards of what is "right." Look at the political campaigns. Often candidates will try to humiliate the other person by attacking her or his character, saying they're unworthy of public office. Besides using the healthy conscience to free you internally from this shaming tactic, there is also action that can be taken externally. As voters, we can refuse to be distracted by such strategies and turn to the issues involved. As consumers, we can refuse to purchase products that use advertisements such as, "If you drink this brand of coffee or wear this kind of makeup, you're in the 'right' arena or you'll be acceptable and beautiful in the eyes of our society."

As the wild woman emerges, we will naturally challenge such systems of attack. As they no longer become effective means of controlling people, they will have outlived their usefulness. By supporting the heart of the wild woman, we can free ourselves internally and externally of the self-degradation and shaming tactics that a repressive society sanctions.

Fear

Unleashing our wild sides can be a frightening prospect. Think how long we've buried this side of ourselves. It's as though the wild woman has lain in an Egyptian crypt, waiting to be uncovered by an ambitious archaeologist.

The true adventure here is that you can be both the discoverer and the treasure! It takes guts. When I asked women what had kept them from being wilder, they shared many reasons and fears: "What would people think of me?" "What if my wild side changes my whole life?" "I'm too tired." "I have too many responsibilities." "My wild side can wait." "Who will take care of my family?" "What if my wild side leads me astray?" "What if someone disapproves of me or attacks me?"

Women fear that if they get in touch with their wild woman she will take over their lives. But it doesn't have to be that way unless that's what you decide you want. Wild women's desires may be something very simple and easily incorporated into our lives. Then again, maybe the women who fear the takeover the most are those who know that their wild woman has been suppressed for too long and, if let loose, will be out of control.

Now that I've had more experience with my wild woman, the idea of listening to her excites me, but I haven't always felt that way. Our fears need to be dealt with if we are going to allow our wild woman to surface. Fear, like any other emotion, is one to be respected. It can also take different forms in different people at different times. The wild woman may experience some fear or excitement at the prospect of trying something new — an unknown adventure. Perhaps she decides to try her voice at a local talent contest, something which takes gumption. Fear can also be instinctive, like the intuitive self-preservation that the buffalo or deer experience. This includes fear of putting your hand in a fire, or of jumping off a cliff. It is also that gut reaction we get if we are listening. A woman could be stopped on the street by a man and, as the man asks directions, the woman notices that the hair on the back of her neck is standing up. It's definitely time for her to move on. Then, there is the kind of fear that women have lived with who came from traumatic beginnings or experienced a terrorizing experience in their lives. For them fear can be a way of life. Each of these forms of fear is worth discussing further and is, as I mention later, worth discerning one from the other.

Susan Jeffers writes in *Feel the Fear and Do It Anyway* that people generally use the "no-win" decision-making process. They imagine all the horrible things that could go wrong in a situation, and let their minds drive them crazy by predicting a negative future and paralyzing themselves with anxiety. Self-doubt enters in and trust goes out the window.

Jeffers affirms that the alternative to this kind of thinking is focusing on things working out the way you want them to. Talk to people and discover the many alternatives available to you. Then decide what it is you really want to do, not what others expect of you. Basically, trust your impulses. She then suggests moving ahead with your decision, knowing whatever you choose to do can be changed again.

This has quite a bit to do with getting to know and then expressing one's wild woman. Trust your feelings, and if you like what you hear and have a great time experimenting with this side of yourself, then forge ahead. It's not necessary to push yourself if you don't feel right about something, yet consider that not everything will feel comfortable right away. Change and risk can be uncomfortable, but the risk will be worth the adventure.

I used to feel embarrassed climbing upon the twenty-five-cent metal horse in front of the supermarket and then pretending I was riding a wild horse while hollering, "Ya, hoo!" but it is something I just love to do. It's so ridiculous and fun. After I realized that nobody was going to tell me, "You look foolish," or "Hey, that's for kids," I started to do it more often. Now I focus on the fun I'm having, instead of what other people might be thinking.

Opening up to the wild woman can be both frightening and invigorating. If I want to weigh the consequences of being wild in a situation, I simply ask myself, "What can they do to me? Lock me up? Be rude to me? Criticize me?" Those are things I've already done to my wild woman. When you do something outrageous, most of the time people will either join in on the fun or leave you alone. If people are critical or rude, they are simply projecting their own shadow sides onto you — in other words, it's their problem.

Margie had never gone out to dinner by herself. She felt too self-conscious. Her internal oppressor told her, "People will think you don't have any friends. It's better that you stay home." She was tired of cooking every night and wanted an evening to herself, so she listened to her healthy conscience who told her, "You'll love eating out alone. Other people are busy with their own lives and won't even notice you're alone." Margie dressed up and went out to dinner. Although she admits it was uncomfortable at first, eating out alone has now become one of the things she really enjoys doing for herself.

The self-doubt and fear, such as Margie experienced, is very different than the intuitive, instinctual fear that is like that felt by wild animals. This is not the same as the excitement you feel before trying something new. This is not the same as the anxiety you feel when you listen to your internal oppressor. This fear is the healthy, protective response of human beings which combines instinct with intuition. Though we alone possess a conscience and the power of analytical thought, we are, after all, mammals. If you suddenly feel frightened or anxious, then your heart and mind are trying to give you a warning. This feeling of fear may be letting you know that the stranger you're talking to is not safe, or that your usual way of walking home should be avoided tonight; take another way home.

Once I was working on a particularly unpopular story for a small town newspaper. I'd gotten bored with my regular beat — the courthouse, school board and so forth — so I'd begun to dig under covers that some people would have preferred to have left untouched. The newspaper had received a few threats, but nothing that seemed too serious. One night I came out of the newspaper office and, for the first time in two years, I felt I should drive along the main road to my home instead of my usual back-road shortcut. Halfway home I ran out of gas. I got out of my car and noticed my gas cap was missing. Since I had filled my car with gas earlier that day, I realized someone had siphoned my tank. Someone I knew drove by and took me home. I often wonder what would have happened to me if I had ignored my instincts and had run out of gas on that lonely, dark back road.

If we listen to our feelings, many dangerous situations can be avoided. As wild women we want to become more finely attuned to our inner voice.

Many women experience the fears I've mentioned, in addition to something more painful to live with: fear as a way of life. Most of these women grew up from traumatic beginnings, or have experienced an event of terror that has caused them to live with a constant need to be on the alert. They wake up scared and continue through their days feeling scared. A noise or an unknown event can set off fear that automatically runs through their whole bodies, leaving them shaking for hours. They fear people, places, trying something new. They fear the dark, the light, and suffer from a free-floating anxiety they can't give a name to. If they were really honest with themselves they'd probably admit to not having a day free from this fear. When one grows up in traumatic surroundings, or has experienced trauma, the "fight-or-flight" response becomes automatic. The boss calls you into the office and immediately adrenalin is pumping through your body. Before you have a chance to hear what she or he has to say, you assume that something very wrong is going to happen.

This kind of fear needs to be treated holistically (like anything else). Biochemically, the fight-or-flight syndrome, anxiety and panic can be treated by a good nutritionist and/or homeopath, or medication from a knowledgeable psychiatrist, in addition to any therapeutic and spiritual support you may need.

For women who have lived at this level of fear, integrating the wild side may be a slower process, but does not need to be excluded. The wild woman can also help with these fears. Just knowing there's a wild woman within can often help one feel safer.

Marguerite says she has always been afraid of everything, even too afraid to say no, so she often gets in situations she would never have tried on her own. She tells a story of how an old woman took her to a two-hundred-year-old church, one which her friends had warned her was haunted. When this woman asked her to come with her she was too afraid to say no, so she prayed for the courage she needed and wanted. To add to her fear, the church was dark inside. In one corner where more light came through the windows, a loom for weaving was set up. The woman took ten or fifteen minutes to show her how to use it and then left her alone in this dark, cold church. She said she was too afraid to get up and leave, so she ended up weaving her first two pieces of work before the woman returned. Marguerite now weaves professionally.

Although Marguerite sees herself as being frightened by everything, I see her as courageous. Perhaps, that day, it was her wild woman within that allowed her to stay and explore her creative side, and the wild woman without that led her to the church.

As Jeffers points out, the mind has a lot to do with our fears. What you think affects your whole being. People have known for centuries that the mind can be a source of terror or of great power and inspiration.

My mind has often been a source of terror. After co-authoring *Living In the Light*, I was sent on a publicity tour. I was to lecture and give workshops. I didn't think anything of public speaking until the tour was set up for me. Then I began to think of all the things that could go wrong. I'd think to myself, "I could suddenly go blank, and people would holler from the audience, asking me questions I didn't know the answer to." I went on the tour anyway, and I not only survived New York and Philadelphia, but can honestly say that, overall, things went very well. That, however, was not good enough for my mind, which kept after me.

When I reached Chicago, where I had expected a smaller crowd than in other cities, I was informed that I was being switched to a larger room than the one I had initially been booked into because hundreds of tickets had been sold. I got sick. I can still remember being on the bathroom floor, praying for courage and phoning friends for support. I thought about calling in sick that night. Finally, I forced myself to dress and decided to walk to the theater. When I arrived, I stopped outside and talked to people who were standing in line waiting to buy tickets. I started having fun. I was no longer alone with my mind. I gave a two-hour workshop and I can't remember what I said. I know that people hollered from the audience that the room was too crowded and the seating arrangement wrong, so we simply rearranged the seating. Then someone did ask me a question I didn't know the answer to, but someone else in the audience did know the answer, so things worked out in spite of my mind. In fact, the sponsors said it was one of the most successful nights they'd had in a long time.

It's important to examine how one thinks and then examine if there is any basis in reality for this thought process. Is it really necessary to worry about losing your job, or a relationship, or dying before you've even gotten out of bed in the morning? Our minds can be our adversaries more often than we think. A woman can look in the mirror and think, "Oh no, one more wrinkle." From that thought she thinks, "I'm getting too old, I'll never meet anyone and I'll end up old and alone." Her mind is literally terrorizing her. It is important to catch the terrorizer in action and refuse to listen to it.

This kind of self-talk was learned by listening to and adopting other's beliefs about you. Margaret shared that she hated the way she looked and, if at all possible, avoided mirrors. She told me that her mother had always told her how beautiful she was, and that others had also affirmed this. In examining the situation further she remembered listening to her mother talk about how she hated her own looks and was always putting herself down, so she avoided mirrors too. Margaret had taken on her mother's fears.

If you discover that you have literally taken on someone else's fears, you can give them back. In my work, I usually have people close their eyes and imagine the person standing before them. In the above situation, Margaret saw her mother. In your mind, you can also choose to talk to the person, telling them what you're giving back and explaining that it wasn't your job to carry their fear. Margaret told her mother that she was giving back her self-hatred and would now attempt to replace it with self-love. Many people are not comfortable with returning these feelings directly to the person, so I ask them if they'd like to return it to the person's Higher Power or to the earth or sky — all of which will know what to do with these unwanted feelings. However, sometimes it's very important to return the feelings directly to the person or their Higher Power because that person may need all of this energy to complete some unfinished business.

Guilt can often prevent people from returning an unwanted present. If you've carried this burden for a long time it may be difficult to give up. The original reason you took on the feelings may have been to help out, caretake or, after being around these feelings for so long, you believed them to be your own! You may want to ask yourself if you're ready to give up these fears or beliefs. You may want to ask yourself what life would be like if you loved and accepted yourself. Just asking this question can frighten some people because they've lived life in a certain way for so long. Letting go of something we've clung to may require emotional preparation. Think about the change, imaging what you would feel like if you changed. Give yourself time. If you choose to give it up, remember to replace the fears with positive images of what you do want for your life.

The mind will basically take orders from you and, for most people, it needs a lot of retraining. One of the best things you can do is to talk to your subconscious mind, saying, "I now direct you to remove any unnecessary fear from my life and replace it with a sense of peace and joy." Do this right before going to sleep. You can then add, "While I sleep, the subconscious mind continues to work to eliminate anything different from these instructions and I awake refreshed and alert."

Visualization is also an excellent technique. You can close your eyes and imagine yourself at peace and relaxed. Get the feeling of that peace as it enters your body, your cells. You may want to imagine what your wild woman desires and see yourself doing whatever comes to mind. Allow yourself to feel the freedom and naturalness that this image brings. Writing techniques are always valuable for dealing with fear. Write out everything you are afraid of, then tear it up or burn it. Subsequently write out all the dreams and desires waiting to be expressed.

There are many new thought techniques to cleanse the mind of the old and retrain it. The mind is happy to take direction. It would just as soon run a first-rate movie as a grade-B one. It's up to you to consciously stop yourself from thinking negative thoughts and replace them with award-winning thoughts.

Living in the moment is a powerful means of dispelling fear. Your mind may be going on about that airplane ride coming up next week or the fear of losing your job. Yet here you are, working in the garden. When you catch yourself frightening yourself, let those thoughts float on by. Focus on what you're doing, or look around and notice what the day is like. Invite your healthy conscience in for encouragement and imagine everything working out well for you. Again, for women with this kind of everyday fear, I suggest taking a holistic approach. Look at how you're treating your body, get nutritional and biochemical support, therapy or spiritual support — whatever you need to free yourself of this burden you've lived with for too long.

The wild woman is within all of us and she can be trusted. Perhaps you'll want to take time to listen to the beat of her heart, and the comfort of knowing this force of power and wisdom is within.

Part of wisdom is discerning what kind of fear you are experiencing. For the woman who has been frightened of everything all her life this will be especially important. I've heard women say that when it is an instinctual fear they'll get a strange feeling in their stomach, or their hair on the back of their neck will stand up, or they will hear the voice of their conscience saying, "Unsafe, unsafe," or "Get out of here." If you're feeling fear, ask your conscience if what you're experiencing is instinctual or a reaction to a past event. Your healthy conscience can help guide you when you are in doubt.

For example, a friend of mine felt safe and excited with a man she had started dating, yet when she was away from him she'd doubt her judgment. He had some physical features similar to her father, who had abused her. Actually, when she thought about it, she realized that many men had similar attributes. She kept listening to her heart while she was with him and, if she felt frightened, she'd remind herself that he wasn't her father and she was not in danger. Both facts have turned out to be true.

If it is excitement at trying something new, you can feel your heart beat with anticipation and feel the wild woman within encouraging you to go ahead and try what you've always wanted to. Maybe you're frightened, but you know in your heart that you're safe and your fear or excitement is natural. Hurray! It's time for being yourself, for those spontaneous urges to surface, for the fun to begin.

Anger

Women do get angry, but ninety percent of the time it is misdirected. Since we live in a repressive society, anger, like other feelings, is seen as something dangerous needing to be controlled. The problem is anger has a way of getting expressed one way or another, usually misdirected toward people we love or ourselves instead of the source of the problem.

For example, Terry was thrown off guard when she was inappropriately approached by a co-worker at the office. Instead of telling the guy how she felt, she held her feelings in. When she got home she screamed at her dog who was in need of her attention. With the dog cowering in the corner, Terry marched into her kitchen and placated her remaining anger with food before collapsing in front of the television.

Many women say that it is easier to express their anger at their loved ones than to confront a friend, boss or co-worker. There is a deep fear of being abandoned, disliked or condemned for expressing anger. Women fear being dismissed as hysterical or labeled as a bitch.

As wild women, we can express our anger in any way that feels right to us. Susan was tired of being so "nice." She thought it wiser to go to her boss who had just promoted a man to a position she expected to be hers and say, "Well, Mr. Hanks, I feel upset that I was overlooked once again for the job I deserved." This time, however, she stormed into his office, pounded her fists on the table and said, "I deserved that promotion, you asshole!" She also threatened to bring in a few organizations to investigate what had happened. In this case, she got the promotion. This could be one woman's style but not another's. We need to find ways to handle these situations that fit our wild woman nature, yet still get our point across. We no longer need to underestimate our power in being able to handle situations directly. The more we accept our anger, the more others will. A woman doesn't deserve to be fired for expressing her anger at her boss. She also does not need to be left feeling abandoned by her lover or a friend for saying what she feels, although I know these things happen frequently. However, this can change, as we become irreverent to the unwritten law, "Thou Shall Not Be Angry."

Some wild women's anger will be fiery and direct, while for others it will be simply but clearly stated. We can build up to a point where we can stand tall, filled with self-esteem and say, "I am angry that I didn't get the job that you know was rightfully mine." Then, if you do not get the response you desire, you can seek out other options. We have been trained to discount our influence and power. If we turn our victimization around, it *will be felt!*

Your anger is trying to tell you something. You could flare up in a situation at the moment, or you may be suffering from stored-up anger from the times in the past when you wished you had said no when you *meant* no, or the times you were victimized and had no choice in a situation. You could be angry at the world situation — pollution, child abuse, mass murders, corrupt government — or, moving closer in, unresolved pain from past events, losses and unfulfilled dreams. In the workplace there is often lower pay and sexual harassment.

In the home, many women are still the primary or only caretakers of the family. To add to all that there's always the barking dog, an unhelpful bank taller, rude drivers, or a neighbor who cuts your tree down by mistake.

So isn't it time we got "good and angry," as my mother used to say? Jump up and down, make noise, let people know what we're angry about! The only problem with this is that feelings of rage and anger cannot always be addressed in person for fear of further abuse, possibilities of being abused ourselves, or perhaps the person you're angry at is dead. But there are many ways to express this anger effectively. Your anger can be used to fuel positive change or healing in your life.

Moving in the wild direction, there are some tools for expressing anger that you may want to try. You may also want to ask for support from friends, a therapist or group, in doing some of the following. None of the suggestions need be done with a sense of "I Should" express my anger in *this* way. If your style is different than what is offered here, then do what is effective for you. However, you may find some of the following just what you are looking for.

I believe Mother Nature and/or the Higher Power wants to hear our rage — who said the Divine likes wimpy people, anyway? So, one option is to go outside, alone or with friends, to a safe, isolated area and scream out your frustrations. If you like movement, stomp and move in any form as you discharge these feelings from your body. As you move you may even take on the form of an animal. The earth, the sky and the wind will absorb and recycle this fuel for its own needs. If there is not an isolated place for you to go to, you can always close the windows to your home, put the music on full blast and scream. For apartment dwellers, using a pillow to scream into or going into a closet is recommended.

I realize that it can be difficult to find a place isolated enough to really break loose with our rage. About eight years ago I was working on a project, but at the time I was so filled with rage that I had to get outside and let it fly or I was going to explode. Earlier in the day I'd purchased a plastic sword at the drugstore. I took the sword and, with a wild look in my eyes, I stormed outside in search of an isolated place. I knew that over the hill was a valley where no houses could be seen, and I assumed no one could hear or see me. I chose a shrub as my target (since then I've asked forgiveness from that shrub) and I began to circle it. I hit the ground and swung my sword as I screamed, "Get away from me, I hate you, I *HATE* you . . ." over and over again. If someone had been watching, I'm sure I would have appeared to be like a Monty Python character fighting off an invisible dragon.

Well, someone was either watching or heard me screaming because suddenly, in the midst of discharging my rage, two very large and heavily armed policemen came up behind me. My healthy conscience helped me to immediately size up the situation. I knew that if I did not appear completely calm and under control, I could easily be taken to a hospital for a psychiatric evaluation. That would cause me to miss the movie I had been looking forward to seeing with some friends later in the evening. When the policemen asked me what and how I was doing, I flashed them a big smile and said, "It was a rough day at work and I thought I would get some frustration out without bothering the neighbors." These terminator-sized men looked at each other, then at me and back at each other, said, "O.K.," and walked away! Ah yes, once again I found myself playing by the rules, but the movie that evening was great and I have since found safe places, indoors and out, where I can let loose.

It doesn't matter if you know exactly who or what you're angry at when you first start yelling. Sometimes we just know we're angry. Perhaps you'll spend the whole time screaming "No" or "I hate you!" or you'll start off with generalities and move on to specifics. For example, "I'm angry at my landlord. I hate my house. I'd like to strangle my boyfriend . . ." If you just keep going the anger will move. For some people no words are necessary, only images, movement and sounds.

If you don't want to disturb people in your house you may want to climb into your car and scream. I have a friend who likes to get on the freeway, roll down the windows, and scream into the wind as it rushes across her face.

Roaring is another excellent way to relieve tension. Put some music on and just start roaring like a lion. The children love it and join in with dance and sound. When I roar, I generally plant my feet solidly on the ground, bend my knees, take a breath deep into my abdomen and let out a giant roar. It's fun. There can be daily things that build up, and a good roar can take care of them in a rush of noise and energy.

Exercise and dance are both excellent ways to discharge anger. You can work out, or run and imagine the person you don't like is being stomped on with each step you take. It's no surprise to me that boxing is the hot new workout for women in cities. If you're angry at someone, or at your internal oppressor, you can imagine them where the punching bag is. Really feel each blow as your fist connects with the surface of the bag. Pounding pillows on your bed will also release your frustrations.

Throw a temper tantrum. Lie on something soft and let your entire body break loose; roll back and forth, kick and scream, pound your feet and hands and, of course, yell out "No!" I once yelled these long-winded no's which shook every cell in my body for what felt like hours. When I stopped, I felt as though I had gotten every last bit of "no" out of my system, at least for *that* day.

As a wild woman, I'm sure you have or will come up with creative ways to express your anger. One evening Mary, who is very dramatic, was out with us for dinner. Iris was talking seriously about the pain she was going through in her relationship. Suddenly Mary pulled out her dinner knife and started stabbing the bread on the table. As she did so she said, referring to Iris's boyfriend, "Look, there's his legs! Let's pull an arm off and pour some salt in the socket!" Pretty soon everyone joined in, avidly dismembering Iris's absent boyfriend. The action got very aggressive and ended up with everyone in hysterical, wonderful, free laughter and release. As one friend who has heard this story says, "Good thing you guys weren't living in the town of Salem during the 17th century." Although I'm sure our friend Iris still needed to talk about her pain, for that evening she was filled with laughter.

A therapist I know said that her group had a glass-breaking night. She asked everyone to bring all the bottles they had, or to go to a second-hand store and buy plates, cups, bowls and glasses. One member of the group had an empty warehouse they could use. The group really let things fly as those bottles and plates hit the walls. They hollered out the names of people and institutions they'd felt victimized by. Later, people confessed that they had at least once in their lives wanted to do this. In a fit of anger, they had wanted to break all the dishes in the kitchen but had always controlled themselves. At the warehouse, they could experience themselves as being out of control, and not worry about causing harm to any other person or having to replace their table settings.

I have a friend who is a physical abuse survivor who, instead of leaving bottles on the curb to be recycled, brings them to the recycling center and smashes them against the bins. She says it releases so much tension that doing the glass smashing has saved her at least two therapy sessions.

It may seem that these exercises take too much energy, yet I've discovered that people get more energized the more they cut loose. I was working with one client, a successful artist whose work had recently come to a stop. She was in the middle of uncovering memories of child abuse and was unable to paint or do much of anything else. One session I encouraged her to go home and draw the memories or symbols of the memories on large pieces of paper. The images were already swimming around in her head, so I thought it would be useful for her to draw them out and be able to look at them. She shrugged her shoulders at my suggestion and said she probably wouldn't get around to it. As it turned out she went home, started drawing and didn't stop. She filled the walls of her studio with her work. She brought several drawings to me so we could talk about them. Her drawings were magnificent and moving. She slowly began to paint again.

We each have our individual way of dealing with our emotions. The examples mentioned above may not be your style, so ask your wild woman for guidance on how she would handle things for you. Some women can talk to a friend or therapist and their anger is lessened. Others can lie or sit down and ask whatever force they believe in to remove or help them accept what they are feeling. It works. For some women, consciously feeling their anger is enough. I've known others who hold their anger, fueling themselves to action. This could be a direct confrontation or, if that's not possible, using their fuel for creative expression. Drawing pictures and then burning them (stomping on them first, if you have the energy) is also a creative way to dispel anger. Letter-writing is also good. Write out everything you've ever wanted to say and then burn it. If you intend to send it to someone, I recommend hanging onto the letter for a few days, so you can re-evaluate, before actually mailing it to the person, if that's what you need to do.

As wild women, we choose how to express our anger. If we listen to ourselves, we'll know what's right for us in any given moment. No matter how we go about it, the important thing is to proclaim it. Bottling up our anger can only lead to hurting ourselves or others. We have anger turned inward, causing disease of the spirit and body, and rage turned outward that can even lead to murder.

Currently, we have women in prison for killing their abusers, women who are trying to get our courts to accept their pleas of self-defense. Perhaps they were too afraid or unable to utilize their anger earlier to get them out of situations which led them to violence and incarceration.

A woman I know who is probably one of the best carpenters around discovered that her lover had been seeing someone else. Filled with rage, she waited until he went out of town and then bolted all of his doors and windows shut. It was quite a surprise for him when he returned to find he could not get into his house. He got the point. He was being locked out of their relationship. There is a fine line between letting our anger out or furthering more abuse in the world. Sometimes our wild anger will erupt without editing or censoring ourselves. We are not always in control, but we need our healthy conscience around to protect us and others from harm.

Again, the power lies in expressing anger at the source and, if possible, in the moment. Yet, we must be compassionate with ourselves. For centuries women's anger has been repressed.

Are we suddenly going to know how to express it perfectly? The one thing we don't need is more "shoulds" such as, "I should express my anger in the right way." At times I've said to friends of mine, "Well, I handled that situation with the grace of an elephant in toe shoes." It takes practice. The more we allow our wild woman to come out, the easier it will be to express what is natural to all of us — our treasured feelings.

"Nice" Has To Go

The Latin word for *nice* means ignorant and not knowing. In Medieval English it means foolish, and in Old French it means both stupid *and* foolish. Is that how you would like to be described: foolish, stupid, ignorant and not knowing?

None of these words describe a wild woman. She is anything *but* nice. That's because she knows what she wants and who she is. When you think of a *nice* woman, what images do you see? Would you use such adjectives as sweet, agreeable and caring to describe her? Although none of these words are negative by themselves, they still tie us into the caretaking or co-dependent systems from which many women are trying to escape. "She's so *nice* to care for him, considering what a grouch he is." "She is so *agreeable* to be with, and such a good listener." "What a *nice* person she is to continue going out of her way for me." Think about the nice people you know. What do they look or feel like? Do they know what they want in life? Is there fire in their eyes? If so, then they probably wouldn't be described as nice. People like Mother Theresa, Josephine Baker and Elizabeth Kübler-Ross did or do a lot in the world, but I would never use the word nice to describe them. They know exactly what they're doing and how to accomplish what they want.

A symptom of being *nice* is people-pleasing. Some people feel afraid of being disliked, so they go overboard in their efforts to make other people like them. They feel that if someone doesn't like them it could mean they are inadequate, which could lead to abandonment. Most nice people are, deep down, trying to meet their own needs, although they are doing so in an indirect way. "He won't leave me if I don't say anything" or "I won't lose my job if I work late." Most caretakers are so busy scrambling to meet the wants of others that they've never learned how to directly take care of their own emotional needs.

Many children learned this caretaking as a means of survival. For example, "If mom and dad are happy and not abusing each other or drinking, I'll be O.K., so I'll be even better and I'll fix things, so then they'll be happy." Often children's needs are forgotten in the midst of family dysfunction. The child is afraid to feel her or his needs, because they don't want to be an added burden to their parents, or they know, through experience, that their needs won't get met anyway. Because of this, it becomes easier for them to focus outside themselves than to feel their pain.

As adults, there's nothing technically wrong with people-pleasing. The problem comes when being *nice* is still motivated by the past pain that got shoved down into one's shadow; that desperate need to be loved and wanted. It's difficult to face the idea that desperation could still be your motivation. Yet once this is confronted, you'll know what your motivation is and can then decide whether you want to follow through or not. Remember: we don't have to be perfect.

We have all bought Girl Scout cookies when we knew we wouldn't eat them, or let someone go ahead of us in line at the grocery store because they had fewer items than we did, or have stopped to help a motorist whose car has broken down. It's not the action taken, it's the effect is has on our hearts. It's easier for us, in the long run, not to give out of desperation or obligation.

Cheryl was asked to make yet another visit for dinner at the home of her lover's parents. On her first visit this elderly couple had said, upon meeting her, "You look so normal." The evening had gone downhill from there. Laura's parents were convinced that this woman had corrupted their "little girl's" life. It had been months and Laura, in an effort to please her parents, had convinced Cheryl to give it one more try. She promised Cheryl that her parents just wanted to get to know her. The last thing Laura had said to Cheryl as they rang the doorbell was, "Now, try to be *nice*." Whoops! Cheryl *did* try to be *nice*, but as the evening progressed, the anger grew inside of her. The final straw was when Laura's parents brought out a photo album which included pictures of Laura's wedding day. They told Cheryl what a great guy Laura's ex-husband had been. Then Laura's mother, thinking all was going well, bent close to Cheryl, held her hand and said, "Dear, you're so beautiful. I'm sure you could find a *nice* man to be with." That was it! Cheryl jumped up and grabbed her coat, with Laura following her, and said, "Until you respect who I am and the relationship between Laura and me, I don't want anything to do with you."

Cheryl admitted later that trying to please Laura by going to see her parents again had only brought her emotional abuse and led to a big fight about what bigoted old goats Laura's parents were. So much for trying to be *nice*.

I hope if people have called you nice, as they have me, you won't feel insulted by this section. It's too easy to take a table in a noisy section of a restaurant instead of asking for the one you want, or to overlook your boss's overt comment, hoping it will remain an isolated incident. Learning what we want in life and how to take care of ourselves takes time. It's been ingrained in many women to be nice at the cost of our own welfare. It's a process of recovery for us to listen to our wild hearts and then follow what we hear. One won't necessarily go from nice to uncaring, but some wild women will initially need to do just that, while others will find themselves somewhere in the middle. The important point is to learn how to say no when you don't want something, and yes when you do.

As our wild woman surfaces, we will find our communication more direct and assertive. We do not have to suffer the "Well, I don't know — O.K." syndrome. Being clear and direct is honest. You may feel guilty at first, as you begin to do and say what you want. That is a common reaction to changing an old pattern.

I've heard people say, "Well, isn't it selfish to just do what you want? After all, I want to be a nice person." When following the guidance of your natural, wild woman, you will still be giving to others, but you will be giving from the heart. A gift from the heart is felt ten times more than a gift that is given out of duty, or from your own needs. Your needs can lead you to be nice to avoid guilt, confrontation or abandonment.

Your wild woman knows freedom through direct behavior. Being nice can only end up getting us in the grips of a caretaking or co-dependent relationship. This leads to unhappiness in the long run. One or both people generally feel resentment as time goes on.

Jennifer used to be so *nice* that she didn't know how to say no to anyone. Finally she had to learn how, because her list of resentments was building. She was spending time with people she didn't really want to be with. Her close friends were last on the list, instead of first, where she wanted them to be. She was gradually handling the situation and learning to be forthright. Yet one powerful woman, who must have reminded her of her mother, kept hounding her, asking when they could get together. Instead of being direct with this woman, Jennifer was trying to be nice by giving hints, but they weren't working. Occasionally she'd end up spending time with this woman out of a sense of guilt.

One day Jennifer couldn't take it anymore. She had become so angry at herself, and resentful of this woman, that she decided to call her up and be honest with her. She paced the floor, took ten deep breaths and called her. Jennifer got right to the point by telling the woman that she didn't have time to spend with her, and that she found it very difficult to say no. The other woman was hurt and angry that Jennifer felt the way she did and had waited so long to tell her. When Jennifer got off the phone she felt guilty and sick to her stomach. She learned that if you mean no, say no. It will save a lot of time and energy. Over time, she began to sense how she felt more quickly, saying what she meant. Not being so *nice* became much easier for her.

Guilt

Guilt is one of my *least* favorite words. It comes right after guillotine in Webster's Dictionary. It means, by definition, that you've committed an offense or done something ". . . deserving of blame or punishment, legally judged an offender."[7]

What a weight. No wonder I don't like the word. Our internal oppressor loves guilt. It tells us we've done something wrong or been offensive whenever it really wants to control us and keep us in further captivity. If we're going to change, which we will as our wild sides emerge, then we may feel guilt. This is because we're so used to traditional roles. But, if you examine the definition of the word, you'll discover that you do not need to feel guilty. You haven't done anything wrong, you've simply changed. Yes, if you purposely run someone over or abuse your child or partner, then guilt is the appropriate feeling. However, if you're exploring your wild nature — challenging the system — then you may feel guilt at first. You may even ask yourself, "Did I do something wrong?"

I had a client, Sue, who told her husband that if he came home drunk one more time, she was going to throw him out. When he came home drunk, she pushed him out the door, packed a bag of his clothes and threw them out after him. He slept in the park that night, and called her the next day asking to return home. She refused, saying that if he didn't get help she wouldn't have him around her any longer. Sue felt guilty for this and doubted her actions. "Were my actions rash? Was I wrong in what I did?" A week later she received a call from him, saying that he had entered a treatment program. Later, she felt guilty when she thought that maybe she should have done this sooner. Oh well, so much for the negative voice — let's send *it* to the guillotine!

Samuel J. Smith, the author of *When I Say No I Feel Guilty,* states that we grow up with rules that are indoctrinated into us. "Oh, you're such a good girl for keeping your room clean" or "You're bad for not coming when mother calls." Smith writes, "Not only does mom or dad's manipulative control of your emotions and behavior train you further in the arbitrary use of ideas like right and wrong or fairness, but with the same words, your parents are conditioning you to think according to vague, general rules that 'should' be followed. These rules are external to your own judgment of what you like and dislike. They tell how people 'should' feel and behave toward each other, regardless of the relationship between them."[8]

Today, many of us are still reacting to an old set of rules — if I don't do or live the way my parents did, or society expects, then I've committed an offense. We have moved further and further from our own truth.

Think how you feel if a close friend asks to borrow your car, and you really don't want anyone else driving it. At first you hesitate, maybe say yes, and then worry about your car. Or you say, "No, I'm not comfortable letting someone else drive my car" yet you feel guilty — like you should have done something differently. Have faith, it gets easier.

The wild woman, the true, natural you, is sure to challenge the oppressive rules, so be prepared for some feelings of guilt. Again, they will pass with experience. The more you let this wild, uncensored self out, the less guilt you will feel over time. You can also cheer yourself up by reading Webster's definition of guilt, and know you are really not ". . . deserving of blame or punishment and legally judged an offender." You simply and courageously said no to a friend, or decided not to visit the family for the holidays.

Identity Change

When certain women uncover their wild woman, there's no stopping them. They've finally broken loose. They say, "I've had it and won't take it anymore." Huge, swift changes are then made in their lives.

A friend of mine, who became irreverent to her old repressive rules, left her family, bought all new clothes, and went to Europe to study with a famous opera master. She said it was never too late to do what we really want in life, and that it was time her husband supported her art (after she'd put him through law school). She said the children were old enough to be without her for a while. Her friends and family felt it was a rash move, yet some of her friends told her they wished they had the courage to do the same.

Another woman I know had an affair during her marriage, changed careers, got a tattoo and began driving a motorcycle. She said as a result of these changes, she had never felt or looked better. She was so tired of being a mother to her husband that she just had to break out of the mold. Some women have felt oppressed by themselves or others for so long they almost fear that if they don't make the move now, they never will.

A quality both these women have in common is an internal solidness. Some women make sudden moves to escape current situations and they're thrown unhappily off balance by the changes that follow. If one is going to make rapid changes, it's good to have your emotional state on solid ground and know who you can count on for support. That is what carried these women through. They were able to make contact with their wild woman for strength, and friends for support, to see them through the dramatic changes that followed.

Each woman will react differently to the changes of integrating the wild woman. Some will move at the speed of a race car; others will move more slowly or somewhere in between. The movie, *Shirley Valentine*, gives us a picture of a woman who made a very necessary change in her life. She leaves home, where her husband's rare words to her are, "Pass the potatoes." She goes to Greece, takes a lover, decides to stay, realizes the romance was only a week-long fling, but that underneath she wanted to be on this beautiful island. Here, she uncovers more of the real Shirley Valentine. Surprisingly her husband, who has been doing a lot of thinking himself, comes to Greece to spend time in her world.

Women I've seen that have changed everything at once are those that needed to do it that way. They had felt so repressed it was now or never. When they let their natural uncensored self come out, they moved forward to have a life that they chose. Perhaps it doesn't turn out to be all of what they'd dreamed, but these women have the stamina to make adjustments and bounce back. This has increasingly to do with inviting the wild woman into your consciousness and listening for her guidance. It has to do with having faith in a spiritual force, which your wild woman is connected to.

With the big changes come doubts and facing the losses in life — loss of some friends, perhaps a partner, a home. It takes the psyche time to integrate these changes and new behaviors. Along with this new freedom comes a need for our inner self to work things out. Also, be on guard, for no doubt our internal and external oppressors will have something to say like, "What are you doing? Have you thought of anyone but yourself? Is this new life practical? Don't be foolish." That's when our healthy conscience needs to step in. We can choose to turn away from our repressive voice and ask for guidance from our wild woman. There will be external matters to attend to, depending on your situation — money issues, partners, job changes, children — all which can be important and stressful when you're in the middle of things.

Angie said to me, "I can't believe what I did. I went to a blues club alone, picked up this guy, made out on the dance floor, and now we're getting involved!" She said, "I'm having so much fun, I've never had the courage to do anything like that, but I wonder if this is really me. I never did anything like this sober before. For once, I let all the old rules go." Angie has fresh energy about her. Her sexual energy has blossomed. She's become even more assertive at work. Letting out her wild side in one situation has freed it to move into other areas of her life.

The wild women I have mentioned are ready for big changes in their lives. They also knew it was their time. So, although there is loss, the gain is so much greater that they are willing to walk through the fire.

If you're contemplating a big change, you'll want to consult your healthy conscience, and perhaps friends and/or a therapist. A woman who is working through some difficult abuse issues and who needs the support of her friends, group and therapist may not choose this same time to travel to the jungles of Ecuador to help save the trees. That could, instead, be a goal she may pursue in the future. Now, a priority for her wild woman can be to guide her through her feelings and grief of her past. She can dance a fiery dance of anger, or scream until she can finally cry. She could join an environmental group near home, get involved, speak out — all of which can be healing for her soul. Yet, to be my own devil's advocate, perhaps I'm suggesting playing it too safe here. After all, the wild woman knows so much about healing that she may know the jungle is just the place for this woman. The atmosphere there could work its magic on her and she would find herself renewed in a way that Western psychology cannot offer. We've suffered so many rules already, we don't need more rules to follow about being a whistling woman.

Some women's wild sides have them breaking loose in a different fashion. They'd like to experience more freedom so they begin to integrate it into their daily lives: going swimming naked in a river or lake, diving off rocks and bridges, dressing flamboyantly and going out to a club they've wanted to try, or suddenly creating a sculpture as in "A Prayer for Sex" in *Stories From The Wild Side*. At the center of this is letting yourself feel more out of control in situations, looking for the miracles instead of the disappointments and having the courage to live in the present.

It's up to each woman how she wants to welcome the wild woman into her life. For me, sometimes I've moved like a hurricane and at other times I've moved slowly. It depends on how happy we are with our current life — do we need a total change or do we simply need more uninhibited fun in our lives? At the core, what the wild woman wants to give us is that wondrous natural state of being, that laughter and humor many women have lost touch with, that self-love and trust that keeps us feeling strong and safe in the world. If gaining this means loss of our old way of being, then it's time to say good-bye to the past.

When we say good-bye to one thing, there will be grief. Yet, if we can learn to frame our grief as a transition into a new way of living, it will become easier to accept.

Chapter 3 Footnotes

[1] Hahn, Thich Nhat. *The Sun My Heart.* Berkeley, CA: Parallax Press, 1988, 17-18.

[2] King, Laurel. *Women of Power.* Berkeley, CA: Celestial Arts, 1989, 166.

[3] Kavanaugh, Philip, M.D. *Magnificent Addiction.* Lowerlake, CA: Aslan Publishing, 1992, 113.

[4] Alcoholics Anonymous World Services. *The Big Book of Alcoholics Anonymous.* New York: AAWS, 1939, 63.

[5] Holiday, Billie. *God Bless the Child.* Universal City, CA: MCA Records, Inc., 1988.

[6] Davis, Laura and Ellen Bass. *The Courage to Heal.* New York: Bantam Books, 1985, 105.

[7] *Webster's Ninth New Collegiate Dictionary.* Springfield, MA: Merriam-Webster Inc., 1990, 541.

[8] Smith, Samuel J. *When I Say No I Feel Guilty.* New York: Dial Press, 1975, 17.

Grief — The Transition

We hold pieces of grief within our hearts so they can tug at our spirits. There is so much to grieve — the lives we haven't led, the words we wished we had said, lost loves, lost childhoods, the souls of our sisters that have passed, fighting so that we could have a better life. Grief that the better life may not have been to be equals in a male world, but natural, instinctual, creative beings: the wild woman.

There's no right or easy way to grieve. As author May Sarton wrote, "It is not absurd to feel such grief. I am undone."[1] When I read great writers of the past and present — Virginia Woolf, George Sand and Alice Walker — or I hear the songs of Billie Holiday, Aretha Franklin and Bonnie Raitt, I realize how they pour forth their passion, their grief. French author Marguerite Duras writes in *The Lover*:

> "One day, I was already old, in the entrance of a public place a man came up to me. He introduced himself and said, `I've known you for years. Everyone says you were beautiful when you were young, but I want to tell you I think you're more beautiful now than then. Rather than your face as a young woman, I prefer your face as it is now. Ravaged.'"[2]

Our society does not acknowledge grieving. I can almost hear Joseph Campbell asking, "Where are the wailing circles? Where are the dances of sorrow? Where are the rituals of death?" In our society we are encouraged to get over our grief, instead of feeling it. Fortunately, this is changing some, but as a whole it's still the old "take a pill," overwork, do anything to make the pain go away.

I remember asking my mother how she dealt with the death of her second child. Her baby was very much alive and on his way out when they arrived at the hospital; then the doctors said *something* happened and he was pronounced dead at birth. They left the hospital empty-handed and in deep sorrow. My mother told me that she felt so much pain, but nobody talked about those things then. She was told to just go on with her life. I felt so angry and sad for her.

Many children are taught that the feeling of loss is just something to get over. Often, when children cry over a loss, the parent tries to fix it by distracting them. Often, because the parent can't face their own grief, they tell the child to "Stop Crying!" "Stop Feeling!"

Our wild woman can help us grieve. She is our natural self, the feminine, our feelings. We can call on her, allowing her to be with us as we move through the pain. Grief is painful. I am particularly referring to the stage of grief where someone is in great sadness, despair and emptiness. For some, it is as if all life has been sapped out of them and all faith is gone. This is a transition stage. In my own passage, when I could finally let myself move through the fear, panic and anger to the tears, I was on my way to the other side. When I say "other side," I'm not necessarily referring to the death of the physical body, but a death of the old self, the old identity, the part of ourselves that holds onto the shame and the fear. An end to the suppression of our spiritual self and our wild hearts.

It is not easy to get into an emotional state where one will allow these feelings, especially when there are so many ways to avoid them through addictions and obsessions of all kinds. Yet our addictions, which have been our great friends, protecting us from our feelings, now stand in the way of our living fully. They keep our wild woman hidden. For the wild woman to emerge completely, grieving needs to take place. The transition to the resolution needs to happen as it is not something people, or this society, can afford to avoid any longer without crashing completely.

The transition stage can be the most difficult. I compare it to what many women go through in childbirth. In birth transition, many women fear they'll never make it. They scream, "Make this stop! God help me, I won't live through this!" When I've sat with my own grief and that of others, I hear similar cries: "Will I ever get over the past? Will the sadness ever end? When will I feel normal again? What's the use, I just want it to be over." A midwife told me, in reference to grief, that a part of wisdom is knowing that if you or someone near you is in the middle of the pain, it will pass.

In her book, *On Death and Dying*, Elizabeth Kubler-Ross described the fourth stage of grief as feelings of despair, loss of faith, sadness and depression. When Kubler-Ross first sought to understand what the dying felt, she was called a vulture by her colleagues. "You've got a lot of nerve asking the dying how they're feeling," they'd complain, but from her work emerged what is now recognized worldwide as the five stages of grief. The first stage is denial, fear and panic; the second stage, bargaining (oh no, this can't be happening, there must be something I can do to make it stop); the third stage, anger; and the fourth stage, depression. Allowing yourself the time to experience all of these feelings is the transition that takes us to the fifth stage, resolution. Resolution brings acceptance of the loss and trust that life, or death, has something new to offer and, perhaps, even reclaiming the trust in the spiritual that has been lost. Later, Melba Cosgrove, author of *How To Survive The Loss of a Love*, was one of the first writers to show how we can go through these five stages in any situation of loss. For example, a friend cancels a date, a breakup in a relationship or a disappointment at work can cause us to feel the same fear, anger and depression.

I dreamt that I walked into my friend's home and saw her dismembered hand on the floor, then her chopped-off foot. I followed the trail of body parts to her daughter's room where I saw a blood-stained sheet hanging from the ceiling filled with what I assumed were the rest of her body parts and possibly her daughter's. I screamed, ran from the house to the neighbors next door and asked them to call the police. I went in the back yard where I screamed and howled, pounding on the grass, praying. I sobbed and shook and screamed some more. In this dream, I saw the paramedics coming toward me with a needle full of something they were going to use to deaden my pain. I ran from them screaming, "Won't anybody let me grieve?"

I woke up shaking, but I knew the answer to the question in the dream. I needed to let myself grieve. Three friends had recently moved (one to Paris, one to Canada and one two thousand miles away). This had all happened within a month and I didn't seem to have much time to feel it. I'd been angry and depressed on and off, but I attributed that to overwork. The dream had served its purpose. I had to slow down and let myself feel the loss of their daily presence. Instead of adding my loss to the pieces of my wounded heart, I could set them and myself free.

We need to give ourselves the gift of mourning — the time to feel our losses. Today, many people are grieving a childhood they never had. They begin by denying there ever was a problem, yet they can't figure out why their relationships or life have been so rough. Then, when they start to experience the fear and panic as they face the truth, people will often do whatever they can to avoid the feelings. When nothing seems to work, then the rage pours forth. All the anger at what really happened to them and how they have had to lie to themselves to keep going is finally revealed. After the anger lessens, the fourth stage of grief follows: depression and/or lack of faith in anything. Finally, when one moves through this transition stage, a sense of resolution can follow.

I've seen people get stuck in certain stages of grief for years, maybe even a lifetime. They'll say, "I've been angry and/or frightened all my life. Are these the only feelings life has to offer me?" This is a sure indication that something traumatic happened to them and they were never able to work it through, or that growing up they lived in the daily dysfunction of fear and trauma and have not found a resolution. If you feel that this is happening to you, then you may want to work with someone who can help you discover the source of that pain, and move into a new way of life.

A friend of mine, who had been in therapy for eight years and had been working on his childhood issues, looked at me one day and said, "No matter how much work I do on myself, I'll never get my childhood back." He was feeling despair and depression, and said those feelings kept pulling him back through the stages of grief. Yet, now that he knew what was happening to him, he could begin to move toward acceptance; acceptance that he could never go back and relive the childhood he deserved. He would not forget what happened to him, but he could now choose to live with the truth and move forward.

Making the transition into resolution can take many forms. Beverly's friend, Kathy, was dying of cancer. She and her women friends had been experiencing the grief process, and it was deeply painful for all of them. Kathy, over time, had moved on to acceptance. More than anything, before her death, she requested that all of them go to the beach and spend the weekend in the kind of joy they had shared so much of. Everyone agreed. Beverly said it was not a time without pain, yet they were able to all laugh and cry about their lives together. Beverly said her friend had taught her so much about dying. As Kubler-Ross has said many times, the dying are our teachers.

It's not that situations of loss will ever disappear, it's how we choose to experience them that makes the difference. Are we going to hang onto the wound or, when ready, let the tears flow? The transition through the despair and hopelessness is what leads us to the resolution. It is like shedding skin or pushing out of a cocoon.

Phyllis hired a private investigator to find out about her grandmother's life and who her grandfather had been. Her father had tried earlier in his life to reach his mother to no avail. When Phyllis first began to get reports from the investigator, she discovered that her heritage was extremely sad. The first time she got a report, she cried and cried and couldn't do much of anything for days. Then she got home late one night and there was another report waiting for her. She opened it and the bleak and sad part of this side of her family continued to unfold. That night she was restless.

As more reports came, Phyllis began to choose the time when she would read them, often asking a friend to be with her. She gradually came to accept that she could not change the past. Although she continued to mourn the information she received she was able, with time, to let go of the pain of a past that had always been a secret to her. She had wanted to know of her past and, although it had not been what she expected or hoped for, she now knew what she had always wanted to know. She had information about her family and herself that gave clarity to pieces of her life. She was able, now, to shed some of the past and make new beginnings.

The resolution is regaining a sense of trust in oneself, in a spiritual force, in life. One's self-esteem grows when you can look back and say, "I made it through and I know that with support I can continue to handle the losses in my life." There's strength in building self-trust when you are in deep pain and saying, "I can't take it a minute longer." Now you can look back and know that things do change, and you can trust yourself when you are stuck in the middle of the worst of it. Now you know more about your grief and its whole range of emotions. Life with its share of pain doesn't automatically dissolve, it just becomes easier.

With resolution comes hope, new vitality, an opening into your soul, to the next step. When we fully grieve, we can discover who we are today and enjoy the power of our wild woman. As our wild woman breaks loose, we are faced with the loss of our old ways of being and thinking. We are less willing to be controlled or to control others. We become more of who we want to be, and allow that natural spirit to surface.

Our wild woman can show us what is waiting for us — the spontaneity, the spirituality, fun and depths of being. If we are willing to release the old concept of ourselves as women, we can find what is new for us in the present and look positively toward the future.

Shedding the Unwild Skin

Ritual can be a very positive part of a woman's coming into her own. Just as many Native Americans in this country perform a ceremony to symbolize a young girl's step into womanhood, so can we ritualize the initiation of the wild woman. Once you are ready to allow your wild woman to be seen, it can be very powerful and festive to gather with a group of friends, or alone, to commemorate with a ceremony what is happening to you. Like a snake, you can shed whatever has been holding you back from being your new self — this is the ceremony of "Shedding the Unwild Skin."

Wherever you live, there are a variety of ways to perform this ritual. One desert night, I met with two other women beneath the stars. We found a place in a sandy wash to make our fire. Fire is very important for its transformational quality in this ritual. Dogs, from various homes, simply found us and gathered at a distance to protect and be with us during this special time. We had each brought something that we wanted to shed, something we felt was in the way of allowing our wild woman to emerge. We brought our anger, our grief, our fears, our past and our own oppressive ways. Each woman took time to share what was in her heart. Then she dropped a symbol of her unwild skin into the fire. We danced around the fire, with drums and rattles, in celebration of each woman's shedding. Our laughter rang through the desert.

Later, we spoke of who we were now and our dreams for the future. As the fire died down, we lay on the sandy wash to feel our closeness with the earth, to nature, how we are part of her and she of us. We stared up at the stars until it was time to leave this sacred place. We returned to one of the women's homes in a great mood, ate popcorn, and made outrageous masks out of cardboard, feathers, glitter and cloth. Each mask is a statement of where we are now, and what we wanted to draw into our lives. I have my mask on my mantle. It is beautiful to me. It speaks of joy, fun and wildness.

I find that every instance of "Shedding the Unwild Skin" is done in a unique way. The two things that I feel are most important are that each woman bring a symbol of something she'd like to shed, and that a fire of some sort is used for its transformative power. A symbol of what you'd like to shed could be a letter you've written, a laundry list, an old sock, a picture of someone or of the old you — whatever feels right for you. The fire can be anywhere — if you live in the city, perhaps a friend has a fireplace. You can line woks or pots with foil and use them for burning things in. Sage can be used to purify each woman before and after the ritual. Sage sticks are sold at local metaphysical bookstores or natural food stores, or you can purchase fresh sage and dry it out. Light the sage and allow the smoke to travel up and down each woman's body.

Since as wild women we're learning more about spontaneity and letting go of control, I've found simply inviting friends together, giving them a general idea of what is going to happen, and asking them to bring a symbol of something they would like to shed is enough explanation. Each woman brings her unique gift to the ceremony.

One evening under an open tepee, after we had done our shedding, a beautiful woman with bells on her ankles suddenly got up to dance. It was so extraordinary that we each decided to take a turn. We laughed as we spontaneously used our flashlights to spotlight the event.

If drums and rattles aren't your style, part of your ritual could be turning on the stereo and dancing to Tina Turner and Tracey Chapman or your own favorites, then perhaps dressing up as that wild, wild woman and venturing forth. Each celebration can be different depending on the women involved.

It's also very powerful to do this ceremony alone. Anytime that you feel the need to shed something that is in the way of being fully yourself, it is a good time to write out what you'd like to say, or talk to the mountain, or earth, or your Higher Power, and let what needs to be shed be released into the air.

Women have let go of abuses from the past, of qualities possessed by their mother or father that they have adopted, their grief at the end of a relationship, their old way of dressing, their controlled sexuality, or any way they feel they have been repressed.

One woman who had a small child was so afraid of being a mother because she feared she was becoming her own mother. In fact, she could feel the rage inside her that she knew her mother had. Although she had not acted on the rage, she knew it was there and feared it would grow stronger. She felt the stress of being a mother, a worker, a wife. That evening she shed the abuses she had experienced from her mother's rage, and all the other ways she had become the negative parts of her mother. She even threw an old sock into the fire because it was a symbol of how her mother had taken so little care with how she dressed. I found out later that this ceremony had affected this woman strongly. She had rearranged her schedule, asking for more help from others, so that she could have the free time and nurturing her mother never thought she deserved. She could now take more time to dress the way she wanted and to bring more order into her life.

No matter how these ceremonies are done, they are very powerful and they need to be done in a way that feels safe and comfortable for you. A friend and I were talking about the power each person brings to the shedding. One evening a group of us gathered to shed the oppression we were feeling, then later had dinner together. We had a beautiful, fun time. Then I left town for several days. When I returned my friend, whose house we had gathered at, said, "I've been getting all these phone calls from the women talking about the changes in their lives, in their feelings." Their lives had been affected by this gathering. They felt fresher, more alive, yet unsettled in the changes they were noticing within and without. My friend finally started saying to them, "Did you really think nothing would happen?"

I laughed. Sometimes we think that we're only gathering for fun or adventure, but often taking action like this is felt by one's spiritual force. As so many wise ones know, prayer does work and any form of ceremony is a symbol of prayer.

Chapter 4 Footnotes

[1] Sarton, May. *Journal of a Solitude.* New York: W W Norton & Co., 1973, 187.

[2] Duras, Marguerite. *The Lover.* Boston: G.K. Hall & Co., 1986, 1.

5
Ready or Not Here We Come

We each have a unique wild woman within. Her needs vary, yet she will always carry your spontaneous, uninhibited, intuitive feelings. Some people see personal growth as a bore and discovering anything new about themselves as too much effort. But the wild woman is the one that can lighten your load. Who decided that growth must be painful, boring and hard work? It may sometimes be, but perhaps if you listened to your wild woman, she'd tell you to throw your latest self-help book out the window, put on your juiciest music and take a bath.

The reason for releasing your wild woman is to enjoy freedom, not to increase repression. Repression is a feeling there's something wrong with you — that you need to be fixed. Freedom says, "I'm a mess and don't care" or "There's simply nothing wrong with me, period." Certainly we can come up with something more entertaining to do than pick on ourselves.

As you consult that natural part of your soul — the one that may or may not have had time to express itself — you will uncover many desires. This chapter was irresistible because it allowed me to compile ideas from other whistling women. One woman would say, "I want to dye my hair purple and get a whole new look," and another would say, "A haircut will do, but I'm letting my hair grow out grey."

My wild woman comes to me in varied ways. Generally, if I slow down, take time in nature, listen, I'll reach her. This initial slowing-down period sometimes brings grief for me, followed by a sense of relief and ease. I could stay in that place, but as I am rejuvenated I prefer playing with my family at the beach, dancing at a club or throwing a ridiculous party. Play and creativity seem to follow a period of rest for me. Yet, I have had to learn to prioritize my life, otherwise I've found myself an overworked woman with no interest in anything my wild woman has to say. I've learned that following the instinctive beat of the wild soul makes life much more interesting.

Uncovering Your Wild Woman

One way of getting to know your wild woman is through meditation and relaxation. Stretch out in a comfortable position and close your eyes. Imagine you're some place you love and ask your wild woman to come forward. You may see, hear or feel her. It may take time to uncover your wild woman if she has been dormant. She may not feel welcome having been ignored for so long.

If you can envision your wild woman, ask yourself what does she look like, what does she move like, what does she wear, what age is she? (These factors can all change depending on your mood.) If you can hear her, what is she saying to you? Does she want you to do something specific, or simply spend time with you in rest? If you sense her, what does she feel like to you? Is she soft, vibrant, strong? Some of you may be well acquainted with your wild woman and have regular conversations. For others, be patient; it may take time for you to get to know each other. You needn't try hard, simply enjoy your relaxation. When the time is right, she will show up.

Wild Hearts

We have wild hearts that can never be broken. For many, it has not always felt that way. We've felt stabbed and betrayed, or perhaps we've been the betrayer. Either way, there is a strong, resilient beat at the core of our wild nature. Still or in movement, close your eyes and begin to listen to the beat of that wild heart. Let is grow. Listen like the tribes listen to the jungle beat or the constant rhythm of the Native American drums. Listen to the beat of your soul — your wildness is there. Sometimes images appear. Your wild nature may take you to places you've never been, or revisit the grief of places you have been, survived and need to heal. It can take you to the depths of the earth and back into the world journeying through the past, present and, possibly, the future. Listen to the strength and the courage of your heart, and the power of the hearts that have beat before us. Tremendous strength lies in the beat of your wild heart — let it be felt.

Some people hear their wild woman when they're taking a walk or making dinner. There's no rule as to when or how she'll come to you. Stay open to her presence — her voice can give you the vitality you need.

Daydreams and Fantasies

Were you ever told to stop daydreaming and get to work? Well, guess what: there's no adult around now to tell you what to do. Only your internal oppressor is around to spoil your fun. Let yourself have those sexual fantasies, play out the whole scene, let those juices flow; dream of travel, riding the Orient Express or meeting someone famous like Whoopi Goldberg. See yourself being asked to write a screenplay for a major studio (for at least five hundred thousand dollars) or daydream about having an intimate talk with a friend you miss.

Pretend. You can talk out loud if you want. Watch children playing alone; they talk to their toys or invisible people. You'd be amazed at what will come out of your mouth when you talk to yourself: an entire theatrical production; a resignation from work; asking someone out; a song. Just follow your instincts. Definitely spend time talking to rocks, trees, streams . . . they answer. When I wrap my arms around a big tree, it says, "I love you and will always be here for you." When I sit on this giant stone in Oracle, Arizona, I hear, "About time you came back to earth, you've been off flying about with another idea. Don't forget your body." That old rock and I have had more than one interesting talk.

Water teaches me pure sensuality and all of the above teaches me what my indigenous friends show me: "We must save these holders of the earth for the future ones to come."

Do Only Worthless Activities

Susan King is the wildest woman I know. She was leading an Adult Children of Alcoholics group of which I was a member. I came in and all I cared about was that I had just seen *The Big Easy* — wow, hot — and I wasn't quite sure whether or not Ellen Barkin had an orgasm in that first scene. Well, the group became quite distracted, and we decided to go to the late showing of *The Big Easy*. There a group of seven or eight of us sat, waiting for this scene. After the scene I hollered out, "Raise your hand if you think she came," and besides our group, half the audience joined in. As I remember, it was a split vote.

Other worthless activities, besides voting on an orgasm, include never reading anything that has to do with work. Read fashion or movie magazines or, something more sophisticated if you must, like the *National Enquirer*. Blow bubbles in the front yard. Just lie somewhere and do nothing. Watch the clouds go by. We're far too worthy and hard-working a society. It's simply part of the repressive plot to keep us in our place. Watch teenagers for ideas. They're right in the middle of rebelling against the system — they're striking out against the oppressor. They're giving it one more stab before they succumb to what we call "social responsibilities."

My teenage research is limited to a large town in the San Francisco Bay Area and a small town in northern California, so your experiences may be very different. At lunch break, these kids seem to fall together into groups and head for the local market. They purchase sodas, gum, candy bars, play video games, read movie magazines, chew lots of gum, and continually bump into each other. They're not afraid to make out in front of the market, or just hang on to each other. When they pull out the cigarettes, they barely attempt to be unnoticed. They can also be seen blowing up rubbers, especially in Marin County where rubber machines were put into at least one of the high schools. Rubber water fights are also fun on hot days. If drugs are being passed, which is certainly happening, I missed that. After school, they jump into their cars — again clumped together — and make lots of noise. You don't have to approve of any of this, but your wild woman gets the idea: it's O.K. to make noise, have water fights, bump into each other's bodies and make out in front of the market.

Taking Care of Your Body

The first thing that is important is to notice that you have a body. This is very easy for the sensual woman — aware of what her body feels like in clothing, while eating, while making love.

There are others who are more cerebral. They're off on some project or working hard at a corporation, and haven't had time to notice if they're tired or hungry until they drop into bed. Then, there are those who suffered a trauma in their life — child sexual or physical abuse and, as adults, rape and battering. As frightening as it may be, part of the healing and the nurturing is returning to your self. Instead of ignoring your body, respond to its needs.

Since your wild woman is naturally sensual, she can help you become more aware of your body. You can begin by looking at your body parts — oh, there are my feet, my arms, my face — and imagine that you're taking all the energy and creativity you have given out that day and bring the positive energy back to your body. Your body needs attention. This takes practice for those not used to noticing their bodies or those who reject their bodies due to self-image. Women often think they should be a certain weight or stature. In most cases that's society's problems, not yours.

Thanks to modern media, people are becoming increasingly aware of the need to nourish their bodies by eating a healthy diet. The problem is whom and what to believe. Studies have been done proving that a lifelong depression has been cured by a missing nutrient. It is important to become thoroughly informed about the nutritionists, herbalists or doctors in your area that specialize in individual needs. We're all unique, living in a variety of places, so when the American Medical Association says we all need this much of that vitamin, or sixteen ounces of this, it doesn't take into consideration the person or the environment you are living in. If you suffer from mood swings or aches and pains, give yourself the huge gift of getting knowledgeable nutritional, medical or herbal information.

To nurture and take care of yourself, the following suggestions were at the top of many women's lists:

- get a massage

- visit a hot spring

- get a facial or haircut

- lie in bed reading your favorite book

- have a spa day with friends where you massage each other's hands, feet and bodies, and give each other facials or haircuts

- play with a child in the sandbox or at the beach

- rub your feet with oil or your whole body with lotion

- sit in front of a fire

- have a friend hold and rock you, or lie your head on her or his lap and have your face touched and fingers run through your hair

- pray and meditate

- take hot baths

- go to beautiful places and bring back the images in your mind

- visit the library and check out videos on beautiful places, animals and/or inspiring people

- seek therapy with someone who nurtures your soul

- lie on your friends' tummies and laugh

- have your favorite meal alone or with friends

- sit with your feet in a stream

- put your hands or entire body on the earth and feel it

- check out your favorite video, wrap a comfy blanket around yourself, unplug the phone and enjoy!

Sensuality

Sensuality and the wild woman are inseparable. Living a fully realized existence is sensual. Freshness is sensual. The wild woman does not criticize her body. She is simply herself.

Think how free of oppression children are. They explore themselves and others through their senses. They reach for a person's face, touch the fur of an animal, smell the flowers. They feel the ocean breeze and enjoy the sensation of grass running through their fingers. If you have lost the ability to feel such things, you can recapture it. We can learn to be more sensual by shutting off our busy minds, living in the moment, allowing ourselves to hold a friend's hand or, perhaps, even touch their face.

Sensuality shines. It's that look one sees when a friend is in love: her skin glows, perhaps she starts to dress differently, she laughs more. The same thing happens when we fall in love with ourselves; after all, self-love is wild in a society that has taught us to dislike so many things about ourselves. If we don't have the "right" job, enough money, wear this season's fashions, meet this decade's body standards, then we do not fit in. Also, how our parents responded to our childhood exploration and whether or not we were given the grace to feel, will reflect in our current sensuality. Some women are not even aware of their bodies, whether or not they are hungry, need to be touched or slow down. It's easy in our repressive world to find ways to ignore ourselves.

Sex

The wild woman can have sex whenever, wherever and however she wants. There is much power that lies in our suppressed sexuality. Unleash it and see what happens. To feel that sexual passion and intimacy, your internal oppressor needs to be sent on a cruise around the world or wherever — maybe a hike up Mt. Everest. Then you can be set free. When most women are asked what allows them to be spontaneous and passionate with their lover, they'll say the ability to be themselves — to feel safe and accepted. Feeling safe is different for different women. Some women feel safer with short-term affairs; they feel free to expose themselves not knowing if they'll ever see the person again. Safety is having no fear of loss.

It can be similar with intimacy. A feeling of closeness and trust can develop in an afternoon for some people, and it is this trust that brings them together in unabandoned sex. They are able to see the beauty in another without the problems that can arise in long-term relationships. Director and actress, Jodie

Foster, was an intern at *Esquire* magazine, where she would entertain herself by guessing if the unsolicited submissions were from women or men. "I was absolutely dead-on every single time," she recalls. "There was this train of thought that all the female fantasies were about, 'I'm on a train, a plane, anywhere. A stranger comes up to me, and he knows me more intimately than anybody I've ever met and says, "I've loved you from the day you were born." We go to this entirely intimate place that I never go with my husband or mate, and then I would get on the train again.' That is the great female fantasy: that you can have this tremendously intimate experience with a very dangerous person whom you don't know."[1]

For other women, the feeling of being themselves with another person takes time and a trust built only through knowing someone. Intimacy is also something that grows, where people know the hidden side of someone and accept them. This is a person you can feel safe to say anything to. Exceptional sexual experiences come when there is a deep love for another that's nurtured through the ups, the downs, the joy, and the challenges shared through time.

The "Stories From the Wild Side" in Chapter 6 incorporate some of the ideas mentioned in this chapter. What is natural or uninhibited to women is truly unique. As friends have read these stories, I found it often depended on their current situation or mood to decide which stories or women they were drawn to. When I think of "A Prayer for Sex" I can envision the most beautiful of sculptures, one that I hope to see again. Some women were fascinated by the get-up-and-go stories or the breaking of societal rules. Others said, "You mean I don't have to jump off a bridge or dance on a table to be wild, I can simply spend time with my children or sit quietly?"

Wild is uncensored, natural, uncontrollable, unrepressed and true to the soul. It's different for each woman, depending on the day or time in each woman's life. Listen to the beat of your heart . . . you'll know what is true for you.

Chapter 5 Footnotes

[1] Abramowitz, Rachel. "Sommersby." Jodie Foster explores "a more private side of me," "Premiere." New York: K-111 Magazine Corp., March 1993, 59.

6
Stories From the
Wild Side

Stories from the wild side are true accounts of women's natural, daring, uncensored acts, and include the birth of a singer, the deep love of a mother and an actress in Los Angeles. You will read of mysticism and the salt of the earth.

I interviewed women across the country — women of different ages, diverse cultural backgrounds and lifestyles. Some of the women chose to use an alias to protect themselves or others. When I first approached women to ask if I might interview them, I heard extreme responses from, "Of course, which story do you want?" to "I have nothing to tell, I've never been wild." For the more hesitant, I described what I meant by wild: a special moment or time in your life when you recall doing exactly what you wanted, without any inhibitions, or a time when you followed your deepest desires and felt totally free. I also asked women to share fun and ridiculous stories, if that's where their wildness lies.

Some women I spoke with knew exactly what they wanted to talk about; others mentioned one or two events and we chose one. Note the age, race, demographics and professions of these women because what is wild to a seventy-five-year-old woman may not seem daring to a twenty-year-old, and what is courageous in one culture or race may not seem that way to another. Yet, there is no comparison. What is vital is the feeling and freedom of being a wild woman, not the result. It's also the immediate action of a wild woman, for if we pause too long to think of what we want to do, sometimes the moment has passed.

What has stayed with me the most is the look on these women's faces as they told me their stories. There was an agelessness, hope, a oneness, a light that filled them.

Some of the women's stories were short — an incident, a turning point — while others were complete journeys. However, I attempted to take the essence of each woman's information and write it into a one- or two-page story. You may want to select certain stories you find challenging, fun or outrageous, the ones that inspire you to let your wild side out. You may also judge some stories offensive, and couldn't imagine anyone doing something so ridiculous or "bad." Both can tell you about yourself. There may be a shadow part of yourself — that wild one who would really like to try what you judge so offensive. Perhaps you'd like to be "bad" just once.

For me, each woman's story is a jewel that I can carry in my soul for hope and inspiration. Here I discover the essence of that strength that, if we, both women and men, acted on our truest knowledge instead of what we have been shoved and molded into, we could make a tremendous difference on this planet.

SARAH BURNHAM
Student, Caucasian, 26, Washington, D.C.

Sex had disappeared from Sarah's life . . . temporarily. She had broken up with her Washington, D.C., boyfriend and had traveled to Taos, New Mexico, to visit her mother. She spent time outside, inside, and definitely, country-western dancing.

One day, a beautiful twenty-six-year-old man came to visit her mother. The only way for Sarah to describe him was to say, "He was pure sex, masculine energy, tall and handsome." He had a strong presence and vitality. Meeting Sarah, he suggested that they go out, perhaps he could take her for a tour of a nearby town. She agreed, and after he left she felt consumed by his maleness.

She was really excited about spending time with him. Then, right before he arrived at the door, her friend said, "You're not going out with him, are you? He's *dangerous*." She had heard he was a fast mover, the love'em-and-leave'em type. Her friend's words stayed with her and, instead of giving into her sexual desires for this man, she pulled back and became cautious and frightened. She made sure he understood this was a completely "platonic" outing. Sarah said he acted like a perfect gentleman, and they had a great time together.

Over the next couple of days, when all she could think of was his pure sexuality, she asked herself, "Why did you keep it platonic? What I'd really like to have done is jump that guy's bones."

The following week she was stuck in the mountains without a car, feeling ". . . completely sexually frustrated, pacing around not knowing what to do with this energy. Then I remembered my mother had told me that sexual energy and creative energy are the same thing," she says.

She grabbed some old boards and chicken wire that were lying about the adobe grounds. She hammered out a cross where the shoulders of a woman would go. "I started molding the chicken wire around it into the form of a woman dancing, one hand raised in prayer. I thought, 'Oh, she's beautiful!' I felt an almost sinful pride and pleasure in her." She originally planned on covering her magnificent sculpture with paper maché or plaster, then thought, "I like being able to see through her. I like being able to see the cross.

"As I was creating it, I knew it was A Prayer for Sex, so that became its name."

DEBORAH COFFEY
Hair Stylist, Makeup Artist, Mother, Caucasian, Mill Valley, California

Deborah Coffey wanted to be the perfect wife but, she admits, it was like being Donna Reed from a dysfunctional family. Well, try as she did, out went Donna Reed and in came Deborah!

She joined a belly-dancing class and became well known as an instructor. She began having belly-dancing classes in her living room. Deborah says, "What I loved best was doing their makeup and hair. I thought about doing it for a living but then thought, 'No way would I do something so natural to me. I'd been doing this since I was twelve.'"

Her husband, hearing of her interests, helped Deborah find the best school for skin care and makeup, which was in New York City. She loved school, and when she returned he helped her open her salon in a prime location in San Jose. "I was extremely happy and the business was a success, but my husband felt threatened." He hadn't planned on the business becoming an independent success.

Although Deborah had been able to put off her husband's request for a child (she already had one child from her first marriage), he was insisting that she give up the business and have their child now. "I asked the advice of the older women in my life and they said, 'Give him what he wants, dear.'" Deborah became pregnant and gradually left her successful business behind.

In the eighth month of her pregnancy, she and her husband decided to go on vacation to Cabo San Lucas. Deborah's pediatrician said, "I'll only let you go because you are going with your husband and he's a doctor. Don't physically exert yourself and stay out of the sun." Deborah says she made quite a picture walking around town eight months' pregnant in Bermuda shorts, wedgy espadrilles, red maternity top, and carrying an umbrella.

Her husband wanted to go sport fishing, so they went down to the docks to check it out. Deborah was appalled. "Oh no, all these dead fish and all these 'macho' men discussing who got the biggest catch." She told her husband he could go by himself — she would surely get seasick.

Then, for some unknown reason, at 6:00 A.M. she was wide awake and ready to go fishing. The men on the boat were shocked and said she could only come if she sat below in the cabin. She was the only woman on board, the rest were crew members or professional fishermen.

"The more I kept watching my husband get tangled up in the line, the more frustrated I grew. I thought, 'What a fool, I could just kill him.' Finally, I couldn't take it anymore, so I stomped on deck and said, 'Give me a pole and help me get some bait on!' He said, 'You have to be kidding.' I said, 'I am going to catch the biggest fish you ever saw.'

Five minutes after I had my line in the water, I hooked a sail fish. They are so strong and powerful that you feel like you are going to fly into the water. I wouldn't let anyone touch my pole. Meanwhile, the crew is pleading to my husband, 'Señor, your wife will have her baby. You must stop her.' He told them there was nothing he could do. Meanwhile, he got horribly sick and was hanging over the edge of the boat. They strapped me down to a chair, and I fought this fish for two hours. When it started to come in I wanted to grab it, but instinct told me, 'Let it out, let it get tired.' When I finally pulled it in, I screamed at the top of my lungs *'Woman Power'* and I knew then that my baby was going to be a girl."

Her fish was seven and one-half feet long and weighted one hundred and fifty pounds. "The kill came out in me, the conquering spirit, I watched the blood gush out." She sent the fish meat home with the crew to be eaten, and had a trophy made out of the skin. "Looking back, it made me feel very powerful. I knew then that anything I decide to do, I can make it happen."

LUCILLE DOLAN
*Writer, Grandmother, Caucasian, 74,
Sacramento, California*

Lucille Dolan can tell of many recent travels and adventures. However, she prefers to tell a story of a time that is characteristic of her whole life.

"We were three North Dakota farm girls, just out of small town high schools. We grew up in the 1920s and 1930s. These were the days of the Dust Bowl, where topsoil and seed blew and blew from state to state and back again. Farmers were

leaving the land and many went as far west as California."
Lucille continues, "I went east as far as my money would take
me, which was to Minneapolis, Minnesota. I would either get a
job or perish."

She found a job and that's where she met and made close
friends with sisters Lil and Vandi. One day, Vandi and Lil
confided to Lucille that Lil was pregnant and her parents would
surely kill her if they found out.

"They had to leave town and I still don't know today
why I went, but I did. I loved Minneapolis. I went to the
movies almost every day. I guess I left out of concern for Lil
and it just seemed like a good idea at the time." So off they
went, walking three hundred miles to Duluth, Minnesota, near
Lake Superior. "It sounded glamorous to me," she says.

"We had very little money between us, so we only ate
one meal a day. We took turns shopping and cooking. I remember leaving with ten cents and coming back with potatoes,
onions and ketchup, and we had all we could eat," Lucille
says.

As they journeyed to Duluth, they were suddenly confronted with a huge bridge overlooking one of Lake Superior's
smaller lakes. This bridge had a ten-cent toll to cross, ten cents
that meant one meal. So instead of crossing there, they decided
to cross on a huge railway suspension bridge. "It was a huge
lake and we were scared. We prayed and told each other we
could do this."

Lucille continues, "We were moving along when suddenly the bridge started to part and the sides swung out to
make room for a ship. We were petrified. We grabbed hold
wherever we could, dangling high above the water, hanging
on with all our might. We screamed, we cried, we prayed. God
saw us and I guess that someone operating the bridge must
have seen us also, because the sides of the bridge began coming back to the middle again. We got up and ran as fast as we
could off the bridge and I never looked back."

Lucille believes that the intense fear she experienced at
that time made her immune from fear, in a sense. "I've stayed
fairly calm in crisis."

Not liking Duluth, they went on to Milwaukee and ended up at a home for homeless girls and women. Lil and Vandi eventually returned home where Lil married the father of her child. Lucille remained in Milwaukee for two years until her brother left North Dakota for Los Angeles. Los Angeles seemed like a good idea, so off she went.

LAURA FREDERICKS
Teacher, Caucasian, 44, Tucson, Arizona

The free, uninhibited, wild side of Laura came to her through a special romance. "Being in love and having someone totally love me in return made this possible. I was loved for who I am. With Mike, I could say or do what I felt. I didn't have to put on airs."

This was a particularly brave friendship for Laura to explore. Her critical background and internal repressor told her she was too old for a man who was fourteen years her junior. She had, as a child, been made fun of for her weight, causing her to be reticent to share herself with another.

Laura says this friendship lasted a couple of years and that it was a beautiful time in her life. They both loved walking, exploring, being outdoors. They'd do things together that brought adventure into one another's lives.

"Once we stayed in this camper in a huge meadow. There was a community of prairie dogs and I sat down to watch. Mike came and watched with me. We didn't have to say anything. In Yellowstone, we were running around laughing and giggling among serious adults. We didn't care what people thought," she said.

"We backpacked in Canyon Havasupai, exploring caves, swinging from branches, then falling into the river getting totally soaked. We walked on the cliffs, didn't have to talk, didn't have to entertain each other."

One particularly uninhibited time she remembers was when Mike was making them an omelet. She started belly dancing around him, surprised at her need to no longer hide her body and her sensuality. She was also filled with joy by his enthusiastic welcoming of her.

Laura says the mutual respect and admiration they had for one another gave her the freedom to be herself. Although their time as lovers has ended, Laura says, "My wild playful side that was lost in childhood has been reawakened by our time together."

SHERRY HILASKI
Mother, Midwife, Physician's Assistant, Caucasian, 41,
Fort Bragg, California

Sherry Hilaski likes nothing better than to don a wet suit and go boogie boarding. She received her initiation into the sport in 1984, at the age of thirty-two, in the cold waters of the Pacific Ocean. She says, "It's fun and good exercise, yet much more than that. It's like a ritual putting on your wet suit, which is the hardest part, then walking into the water and feeling the cold. 'Oh yeah, I'm alive,' I say as I hear the ocean sounds and the breeze hitting my senses."

Besides surfing being a total blast, Sherry likes how it pulls her into the present. "I forget about everything else and become one with the water. You have to for your own preservation. The ocean is very powerful." Sometimes that means floating on your board, diving under the waves, or riding the waves. It can also mean lying on your board and steering, which she says is a very sensual experience. It's like a mentor to her, teaching her to let go of everything else that is happening in her life. "It causes me to face my fears, have trust, and make sure I don't do anything stupid. It shows me my strength. It reaffirms that I can handle things, in and out of the water."

During her first year surfing she was lying in the water, alone, calm, waiting for a big wave, when suddenly she saw an otter swimming near her, playing with her, swimming on its back, around and parallel to her. "I took this as a sign that this is where I need to be and that this is my spirit guide." Shortly after, a friend gave her a stuffed animal — an otter. "My daughter plays with it all the time. This constantly reminds me of the lessons of the ocean.

"Boogie boarding," Sherry says, "is like living in the womb again. When the waves are going to break, a surfer dives under the water, getting into a fetal position to protect their head and back, and resurfacing after the wave has passed." Sherry learned through trial and error how important this can be. The first few times she almost drowned. Instead of diving under the waves, she passed through them, getting stuck in the white water. She says, "It's like a washing machine getting stuck in both the forward and backward motions. My heart rate went way up and the board kept getting away from me. The waves kept shoving me down and I was literally seeing stars. It didn't scare me off, though. If I died doing something fun, it would be O.K."

SHEPARD HILL
Counselor, Weaver, Mother, Grandmother, Jewish Woman of Color, 39, New Mexico

Shepard Hill sees a wild woman as someone "who always walks on the edge, has lots of compassion, takes no shit from anyone, and truly lives by what she has to say. We can all sound good, but it doesn't mean we're living it."

She also says a wild woman is beyond worry about taking risks — she seeks them out. Shepard described what she means by risks. "Initially you learn how to say 'no' to someone, you stand in your own power. Then there are risks about the unknown. I risk by living my life here," she says, referring to the small community around her. "You can't make much of a living, but you have the beauty of the surroundings."

Coming out as a lesbian has been one of the most powerful experiences of Shepard's life. "I'd been working in this leading psychiatric unit and there were a number of gay and lesbian clients whose needs weren't being met. 'This is a test,' I thought. 'Am I always going to be carrying around the names of gay and lesbian centers in my purse?' I was going to have to become clear.

"I had actually gone to the lesbian bookstore in Denver and a woman asked me if I was lesbian and I said 'I don't know.' Yet, I started to see *me* in the titles of the books, posters and the music I was hearing. I was relieved. I knew I had made a major decision that day."

The next day she was driving to work and thinking how she could be of help to these clients. She asked herself, "Am I going to come out at work?" Continuing to sort things out, she then asked, "Why don't I first answer the question within myself: what's happening to me?

"I looked in the rear-view mirror and asked, 'Shepard, are you a lesbian?' I got a big 'yes!' I was happy, ecstatic, my eyes were glowing and bright. I was giggling in the car."

She continues, "I can't tell you stories of bar-hopping or anything like that, because I've only had two lovers. Coming out to me in that mirror meant I was my own lover. That's walking on the edge — I loved myself enough to accept who I am."

Shepard first came out at the age of twenty-six in 1979. She says she is the only woman of color who has come out in the small town she lives in. That has been frightening for her. "I bet the word 'lesbian' has never been in print in the town newspaper, although now they've started a Lesbian and Gay group of AA, which is advertised weekly in the newspaper."

Referring to her town and her lifestyle, she says, "We will never be in the book of great pioneering women, but we ought to, because we are pioneering, we are paving the way." When you're being your true self, Shepard believes that there is a power that protects. "There's a grace that shows in being wild. I don't have to wear armor."

One of the more uncensored stories she told is the night she took off her bra on the dance floor and no one knew how she'd done it. "To me, it was a statement that all my life I'd been told I had to wear a bra. I was celebrating my new-found freedom, my sexuality. In most cultures, they celebrate their womanness; for me, being an American, that was the closest thing to not being locked up."

JANICE EDWARDS
Producer, African American, 26, San Francisco, California

The television show Janice worked on was cancelled and everyone would soon be laid off. It was time for Janice, field producer and assistant director, to find a new job. Through word of mouth she heard about a job at another channel (her station's direct competition) for an associate producer of a studio show.

When Janice asked her executive producer about the job, he said, "It's already been promised and if I were you, I wouldn't even try." Of course, this man had also been the person who had said to Janice, "I thought you were a 'different kind of black person.' I didn't think you would speak up about issues." Needless to say, they did not get along and Janice says, "He blocked any chance I had of getting a promotion and title change at work."

She ignored his response regarding the new job. She worked with her prayer partner, a friend she visualizes, prays and does affirmations with. They decided to get tickets to the show she was determined would hire her. They sat in the audience and her friend said, "Let's just claim this job for you now." Later, she cut out the logo from the afternoon show, made a mock-up business card with her name, phone number, and title of Associate Producer underneath it. She carried this around in her purse as a reminder of her upcoming success.

"I'd drive by the station, see the guard and imagine him saying, 'Good morning' to me. I'd see myself with a magnetic card going into the building. I saw myself working there!"

She submitted her production tape, received a call from the station, and was told that two hundred people were applying for the job. One of them was from her staff and had fifteen years more experience. Her confidence was shaken by that, yet she moved forward.

When she went in for the interview, Tony Robbins, author of *Unlimited Power*, was the guest on the show. As she waited, she listened to him address the power of the mind. He talked about seeing what you want, which reinforced Janice's knowledge to do the same.

She didn't feel the interview went that well, so she made a video in her mind of what had happened and replayed the interview the way she wanted it to be. "I saw him liking me and telling his boss, 'I think we should hire Janice.'"

When she returned from the interview, she felt so confident that when her boss asked her what she'd be doing after she was laid off, she responded, "I don't know, but something wonderful.

"I got a call back for the next round of interviews. They said they didn't have a record of my graduation from Harvard. I started to panic but gave the woman the date; it was just a matter of their finding it, which they did," she says.

Out of the two hundred interviews, Janice got the job. Going against the odds, regardless of what people think or say, is no great task for a wild woman willing to go for what she really wants.

JILL KELLY
Chemical Abuse Counselor, Writer, Mother, Caucasian, 35, Berkeley, California

Jill gave birth seven years ago to the most beautiful baby girl, Madeline. As with many women, childbirth had left Jill with stretch marks on her stomach. After her divorce, these scars made her inhibited about showing her body to others. Plus, Jill had always been a lover of bikinis and was a knockout in them. Now she felt forced to turn to one-piece bathing suits, which just weren't as much fun for her.

One day, finding herself in a wonderful new romance and on the way to Mexico, she went bathing-suit shopping. She tried on several one-piece suits and suddenly threw them down in disgust. She was tired of covering up her body. There was *nothing* ugly about nature's wondrous experience of birth.

Jill dropped the one-piece suits, ran out of the changing room and picked out several sexy, revealing bikinis. As she looked in the mirror, she liked what she saw. When she had chosen a suit, she unabashedly pranced out of the dressing room and modelled this bright yellow and orange suit, which she purchased.

LAUREN MATTHEWS
Writer, Teacher, Mother, Caucasian, 44, New Mexico

Lauren Matthews arrived in New Mexico feeling "old and frumpy" at the age of thirty-nine. she felt the suburbs had smothered her. She and her husband, Paul, had gone from being hippies to his working a white-collar job. Lauren was surrounded by his Irish Catholic family and a life in the Chicago suburbs. "Like a ring around the collar," Lauren says.

Lauren had tried to be the perfect wife. Her husband discouraged her from working so she stayed home, was faithful, made friends in the neighborhood, strolled with their two children to the local park and cooked dinners.

"It was like we had this Norman Rockwell family, but Paul and I couldn't talk about anything that mattered. We lived there eleven years and, through a process of assimilation, we became an upper middle-class family," she says. "I felt my true self was repressed. I felt camouflaged. The only place where I truly felt myself was when I wrote. It was a healthy escape that brought me some degree of success."

Writing or not, she still knew that there was something missing from their marriage. "My husband didn't believe in the spiritual life, so I tried to keep my spirituality hidden in this little place inside me. You can't imagine how ingrained the perfect marriage was, and the longer we lived it the more entrenched we became." However, inside, she knew they were growing further apart. After seeking an answer to their individual loneliness, they thought if they left Chicago they'd regain what they had felt years before. They travelled a while, and it was in New Mexico that they found openness and a beautiful hacienda — their new beginning.

The first day, while the movers were unpacking their belongings, Lauren spotted a young Hispanic man and he spotted her. No words were exchanged. They eyed each other for the next few days. There was something between them that she could not explain. Then, Paul asked her how she felt about hiring twenty-four-year-old Manuel to remodel the house. Lauren agreed.

As the months passed, she and Manuel became close. They would take breaks and talk about things of the heart and soul. "Manuel has a deep belief in God. This was my first spiritual relationship since my marriage," Lauren admits, "although I was scared; his being Hispanic and Catholic." This was a joyous and painful time for Lauren. She struggled constantly with her inner battle to keep the "perfect family" together while feeling this love for Manuel.

When Lauren turned forty, she told her husband about him. "The whole world exploded in my face. My husband threw me out of the house," she said. Lauren experienced tremendous guilt, not being there for her children. "My survival and passion to discover who I was took precedence over motherhood at this time," she said. She found different places to stay and housesit during this time. Manuel was forbidden by his family to see her, and their relationship became the small-town scandal. "A town without pity," she says.

She was alone all summer. Besides the loss of Manuel, there was the loss of her daily contact with her children. The "ideal" family had crumbled and she was seen as the home wrecker.

"I wanted to die and almost did. My husband took me back and nursed me," she said. "I questioned whether society's standards should have stayed in place in my life. Passion can destroy things, it's such a powerful emotion." Yet, Lauren could not stay with Paul, so they agreed on a divorce. She moved out, continued writing and accepted offers to teach at writers' workshops.

Finally, ignoring the moral pressure from his friends and family, she and Manuel were reunited and later moved in together. They both began to move closer to their dreams. Lauren's writing had changed. "Writing became less compromising, more wild. I don't want to say anything unless it is connected to the spirit." Manuel is now a santero (a carver of saints).

Lauren and her ex-husband still have the pains and joys of seeing their two girls grow up, whose house will they be at now, all the workings that divorced families go through. But, it is less painful now. Two years later, Paul married his high school sweetheart who he accidentally encountered, and Lauren and Manuel recently married after being together four years.

Lauren particularly remembers one trip to Chicago to visit old friends. She had sun-bleached golden hair, wore jeans, red cowgirl boots and a leather jacket. She looked and felt ten years younger. When she told her story, a friend bent close to her and whispered, "I wish I had the nerve to do the same."

TRISH O'CONNOR
Producer, Director, Actress, Singer, Mother,
Caucasian, 43, Sydney, Australia

Trish O'Connor had learned to care for herself and others early in life. Her many talents led her to become a producer and director at a young age. It fit her personality perfectly: she could keep running the show.

At thirty-one she was raped. "I was in shock, very afraid. It was like sitting in a separate place from the rest of the world and not being able to connect back. If you could give it a color, it would be a dirty gray. It wasn't until two years later that I realized I hadn't actually seen a color, everything was black or white or gray. If you were talking to me, I couldn't connect with you. That was the first time that I started to realize how distant I was from my own human connection. That is what made me feel really desperate, because I did not know that space, and I did not feel anything other than fear.

"I had no road map. I'd been to therapists and support groups and did not know my way back, and the fact that I might have to stay there was terrifying. Then, I got so worried about all the other people in the world that must be there, because if I didn't know how to get out of it, what about them? I had to find a way back."

Trish's husband said, "Listen, we have got to find a reason for you to live." Trish said, "I had no reason to live, what I had done, had never made me *really* happy. That is when we came up with exploring what my dream had been when I was a little girl." Her husband would ask her, "Didn't you have a dream?" Trish responded by saying she had always wanted to be a singer, but she couldn't sing. "The thought of singing brought up all of my fears," she says. She had always wanted to be a musical comedy singer. Her husband knew just the teacher, called him up and made an appointment. Trish thought, "Oh my God, I can't do this, this is ridiculous! But it took my mind away from the situation I was in and shifted my consciousness to something that scared me more — this step into the unknown."

Fearing that she would back out, she purchased all the most expensive equipment — wand, microphone, music — and then she'd sit and stare at it.

Her lessons began. "I would cry at every session. I don't know what I was crying about. I felt so embarrassed about opening my mouth and these terrible sounds would come out. But it was much more than that. It was the fact that I was singing that made me cry. When I look back, I think that was a huge part of the healing process. I think there are many, many tears in the voice. Your voice is completely connected with your God-self. So when you connect with your God-self, you connect with your heart."

After class, she would take her tape to the ocean and practice. She was beginning to like some of the sounds she heard. "Then I would have the occasional visitor who I would trust enough to hear me squeak out a song. I would be crying and they would be crying. I started to realize that even though I couldn't sing, I could connect with people's hearts," she says.

"Then I started thinking. I am a producer and I could produce a show and put myself in it. Wouldn't that be great if I could pull that off? I could present a really high-quality show, present myself as a singer and, because I am the boss, I would only give myself a couple of songs. I would come on like the superstar." She explains that the sound man and the band covered for her whenever she hit a sour note. "We did some of the best gigs. I was getting paid three or four times more than most singers, and I couldn't even sing." After seven years, she got tired of the whole thing and gave it all up. She was tired of running things. She knew she needed to give up controlling her life and find another way.

"That's when I met the Shaman. I was taking a holiday, walking through this marketplace, and she was sitting there reading tarot cards. She read the cards and said, 'It's been ten years since I met a soul like you. You are to come to my house, I want to train you.'" She studied with the Shaman. Then at some point, Trish knew it was time for her to travel. She put everything in storage and left for the States.

She kept hearing of a place called Taos, New Mexico, where she eventually arrived. Women would invite her to sweats. One night, a subchief of the Sioux Nation was there and they became friends. "He spent a lot of time personally healing me. He did a lot of work in the water, the ancient practices. His grandfather had trained him.

"During the sweats, I would cry and cry and cry and I think I was releasing the child that had been locked away. It would be so hot, I'd think I was going to die. So I'd dig a hole into the earth and put my face in the cold. Then, I swear to you I'd feel the pain of Mother Earth. It was like my pain and the earth's pain mingled and that would make it worse. I would just sob and sob and sometimes I'd come out and sit by the fire and cry for hours."

Two women took her to the hot springs nearby and she was bathed in healing water. "I was giving thanks to the water, the water is my sister, and I was doing a whole ceremonial thing." After time in the springs, the women were wrapped in blankets.

"I got all these flashbacks of being in some ancient Egyptian bath house. My Shaman friend had told me I was a singer in a past life. That was probably the most exciting moment for me because all of a sudden I realized why I was on the journey. If I had been a singer in these other lifetimes, which you can never be sure of, it would explain this desire from a very young age to sing.

"When I finally stood in front of that mirror after going through that whole spiritual journey in Taos, I was so overwhelmed. I looked in a mirror and looking back at me wasn't my face, but it was me. It was like this Egyptian person. It was so exciting."

Last Christmas, Trish sang at the Hilton in Osaka, Japan, and the band did not have to cover for her. She sang deep and clear. She has found her voice.

LISA ORDONEZ
Full-time Mother, Mexican American, 21, Oracle, Arizona

Lisa loves the outdoors, particularly going fishing. She says there was little affection in her childhood. Because of this, she cherishes the day her father took her fishing. He let her drive to the reservoir. They had time alone, time to talk, just the two of them. The only time she remembers her father telling her "I love you" was on his deathbed in 1986. He died of alcoholism.

As a mother of two, Lisa has found it important to show her children the affection she longed for as a child. "I never want them to hurt for anything," Lisa says. "I love their personalities. I learn something from them all the time. Their eyes glow at a tree," she continues. "I see what they see, the beauty they give a rock. They look so hard, look at the sparkles, the circles. With a child's eyes, you can see the beauty."

Lisa had her first child at seventeen. "All I'd known was partying and gossiping with my girlfriends."

Lisa no longer wants the wild life she had with her girlfriends. She has a gifted psychic friend, Terry, who has been a guide to her. "She's taught me to stand up for myself, to say 'no' or 'yes.'" Terry and she also have fun playing cards together and, of course, fishing. "We went to the lake three weeks ago and Terry's grandson was the only one who caught a fish."

Regarding her husband, she says, "No one thought we'd last, but we have. It's been five years now. We drop the kids at Terry's and go for a ride and breathe by ourselves. We communicate. That is what holds a family together. We share all our desires, work at it, talk to each other. Even after five years, something new often will come up. When we fight, it's between us and we always learn from it." They also love to go out to hear a band, dance with friends, go to dinner.

Lisa likes her time alone, too — her walks through the desert. "It's my time to listen to my thoughts. I try not to be hard on myself, to pat myself on the back for what I am doing right."

MONA PERKINS
Administrative Assistant/Office Manager, Mother,
Filipino, 43, San Francisco, California

At the age of two, Mona knew there was nothing "dirty" about her vagina, but she also realized her mom felt differently. She can still remember the sting as her mother would stick her in a basin of water, and soap up her bottom and vagina. "I'd already figured out this was my mother's problem."

Mona never lost her innate sense of sexuality even though she grew up in a very repressive Catholic home. To this day, her mother wears gloves and a hat whenever she leaves the house. Yet, Mona says it wasn't always this way for her mother. In her youth, she was very beautiful, much sought after by men, and received many proposals of marriage. "But, when my father, a military man, met her, he *tamed* her. He was a real tyrant."

Mona admits to being very calculating at the age of seven or eight. "The only way I'd get my way — like being able to go to a party or spend the day with a friend — was to do something special for him." She'd ask him if he wanted his shoes shined or something special to eat. Then she'd get her way . . . it always worked.

When she moved from Texas to San Francisco in the seventh grade, she said it was quite a cultural shock. All the girls wore tight skirts and had their hair ratted a foot high. She was still wearing dresses that tied in the back and had ringlets in her jet-black hair. "Everybody was small like me. I wasn't used to being around so many Asian people."

She learned what the word "sexy" meant when she heard people at school talking about how great and sexy a certain girl was. When she saw her, she said, "Oh, that's what sexy means." She and the girl later became close friends.

In movies, Mona was always attracted to the sexuality of the women like Raquel Welch, Brigitte Bardot and Ann Margret. "When I finally started to buy my own clothes," Mona says, "my mother did not like them, so I'd leave the house and change on the way to school. I'd buy clothes that were soft and felt good to me, and people would say, 'Isn't she sexy.'"

In the eighth grade she started to get "the stirrings." She reveals she'd go into the bathroom at night and put cream all over her body. "Now I know I was masturbating. I was reeking of sensuality."

Before long she had found her playmate. They would ditch school and go down to the beach. "Sex was better than school, any day." She also found she had uncensored rules regarding sex. She felt it was fine to have sex with a few of her boyfriend's friends. Mona got pregnant and married in high school. However, after the birth of her first child, for her the marriage was over.

In her second marriage, she says her husband was always trying to fix her. She was totally dependent on him. He'd tell her what to wear and when to be home. She found herself doing everything for her children and family, nothing for herself. When she couldn't stand it any longer, she began teaching belly dancing and took on three boyfriends. She said her desire for these men had nothing to do with her husband as a lover. It just made sense to her that if you are attracted to someone, and they to you, you have sex.

"I always accepted it as sex. I think this sexuality is innate in me. I believe it's just the way some people are supposed to be. Out of my seven brothers and sisters, only one brother and one sister are like me. The rest are very conservative."

Men are completely disturbed by her attitude. Mona tells just one story of what she has encountered. There was a younger man in her apartment building. Occasionally, they would eye each other. Then one night they found themselves doing laundry at the same time. She invited him up to her apartment while she folded clothes. She said, "You have this look of someone kind of taken." He responded by saying, "But that doesn't mean I'm dead from the neck down."

Mona said, "So does that mean you want to sleep with me?" He turned bright red as Mona continued. "I asked him if he had a condom, so he went down the hall to get one. We slept together and it was really great." She then turned to look at the clock and saw that it was midnight. She told him the sex had been really good but she had to get up for work in the morning. He asked, "So are you dismissing me?

"The next day he came over. He was soft-spoken and polite but wanted all these answers to my life: 'Where did you grow up? What do you do? Do I mean anything to you?'" Mona responded by saying, "I'm really tired, but if you want an autobiography, I'll have it on your doorstep in two weeks." Then she said to him, "Look, I don't have to justify or explain myself to you just because we had sex. It was a really great experience, in the moment, but this isn't what this is about." His desire to control her did not succeed.

Mona says she is not afraid to show her sensuality. "I know what I am capable of being, but I wouldn't walk into a room full of people and turn everyone on. I have control of my sexuality. At work, it is absolutely turned off, but people still perceive me as sexy and that's O.K."

Her sexual encounters have changed since the AIDS epidemic. She has found that she has to like a person and have a spiritual connection to go through what one has to do to have safe sex. She also says, "I've always thought the perfect relationship for me would be another woman or another man in the relationship, a bisexual couple, if it were safe."

She says although her sexual energy is always there, she doesn't always act on it. Right now it has taken a different form. She is learning to play the piano and working out at a health club. "Mostly I have fun no matter what I do. I go out to dinner with friends, go dancing, and work is fun. I live in the moment. There is a difference between living in the moment and being irresponsible."

She has been working as an Administrative Assistant/Office Manager for a real estate firm for many years. She also raised her two children alone after her divorces. Mona believes, "Taking responsibility in your life and living in the moment has to do with spiritual growth and joy."

CARYN REARDON
Computer Graphics Artist, Mother, Caucasian, 39,
Taos, New Mexico

Caryn lived alone in the Tsankawi cave dwellings for nearly six months, and the big events in her life became the sun rising and setting. "I was interested in indigenous cultures. I thought if I lived in the ruins I would gain insight into their lives."

She found her home in a dwelling dug out at the second-floor level of a sandstone cliff. She took a mattress, kerosene lamp, stove, sketch pads and books with her. She would walk to the road in the mornings, four days a week, so she could catch a ride into town where she worked as a graphic artist. Then she'd catch a ride home. She would haul in water and food from the road.

Talking about her time at the dwellings, Caryn says, "All the things I thought I'd do, I didn't. I didn't cook, I ate raw food, didn't read much. I saw the circles and cycles of life, the way the seasons changed.

"The time spent at Tsankawi was a 'radicalizing' encounter with the natural world. I felt I suddenly understood some of the mythological archetypes I'd been studying for years . . . like the Sun as Hunter, how the Sun pursues and chases away the stars at dawn, the depths of Demeter's grief over the loss of her daughter, Persephone, to the underworld as seen in the fall. I realized the great connection of birth and death, and how each creature lives by consuming others, and each death feeds new life. How the greenest shoots grow out of the old dead tree . . . that ancient image of the serpent swallowing its tail seemed suddenly so obvious, simply obvious." Caryn glows as she speaks.

"Even Homer's 'Rosy fingertips of dawn.' I felt the power there. Power like being plugged into a high-voltage plug, but peaceful too," she says. "Living outside in a beautiful place allowed me to feel just *being* was enough, instead of the puritan ethic of *doing* all the time. Encountering and accepting stillness and being was very peaceful."

Caryn says another facet of this was, "I remember feeling myself as a self-contained little energy pack. I realized that no matter how many people I loved, and no matter how many people loved me, I was still this self-contained solitary being. That helped put into perspective the universal yearning for oneness I sense in and around me."

This experience has also left Caryn disillusioned by how people communicate. "What may have happened is I grew into a point of stillness within myself, acceptance, that felt very real, very sincere. By contrast, I felt in the company of others a superficiality . . . artifice, esteem based on wittiness . . . my social contact left me feeling empty and dissatisfied. I remember choosing to stop talking until I could gain some insight on how to make it better. I can't say I've made much progress, other than to stay aware of all the possibilities from moment to moment. It's a constant challenge still."

In the late fall, it became too cold for her to continue living in the cave so she returned to town. Caryn admits that this experience was one of the slower times in her life. What she used to do to experience wildness and vitality in life was to "go after the adrenaline." Being a lover of sports, she would often challenge nature. When skiing in the morning, she would look down the most dangerous ski slope and then jump. She believed, "If I faced death right away, then I was O.K." The more dangerous the sport, the better. She loved to drive her car at the edge of control. "Once I began to settle down, I would still have dreams of driving off the road into the Rio Grande. My body was still giving me the adrenaline that I wasn't giving it."

What Caryn sees as natural to her today is living a slower life. She does computer graphics; raises her child, Veda, with her husband, Mark; and watches the mountains from their hacienda. When time and desire present itself, she creates magnificent pieces of art, sculpture, adorns skull heads and paints.

She made a conscious decision to slow down, realizing that no matter how exciting her life seemed, her need for adrenaline really was an addiction that kept her from discovering the true Caryn — a strong creative woman who is growing to enjoy the peace in her life.

JASMINE WHITE
Actress, African American, 24, Los Angeles, California

Jasmine White had just arrived in Los Angeles, her sights set on being a successful actress. On her first day in town, she picked up a copy of a trade paper and saw there was an audition for a musical. The audition would be held at the Dorothy Chandler Pavilion, which to Jasmine was a symbol of bright lights and fame. When she was a little girl, she'd seen a production there with Rock Hudson and Carol Burnett, and never forgot it.

The audition was for Equity members who sang. "At the time, I was not an Equity member, and I was not a singer, but I could get a few notes out." That, however, did not stop her. This was just the beginning of her big dream and she was going to audition one way or another.

When the man at the door asked her for her Equity card, she told him that she had just finished an Equity play, but hadn't realized she needed to bring her card with her. He then asked her for her sheet music and she responded by saying she'd do something a cappella.

"Basically, I pushed my way in. I was in Los Angeles and I was going to do an audition at the Dorothy Chandler Pavilion no matter what!"

She said some people were lined up in chairs waiting their turn, and she could hear people singing. She had a strong monologue that she planned to do first, then she'd figure out what to do next.

"When I heard this one woman belt out this song, I thought, 'it's time to go now.'" But, instead of leaving, she went to the bathroom to take a few deep breaths and get a drink of water. Unfortunately, a woman in the bathroom was trilling operatic scales. Finally, she left and Jasmine had a few moments to herself — a chance to rebuild her confidence.

"When I got back to my seat I discovered the opera singer was one person ahead of me. She went in for her audition. When she sang her song she was applauded for at least a minute. When she opened the door, they were still clapping," Jasmine says.

Jasmine went in and opened with her monologue. "They asked me questions about performing and I could tell that the monologue went really well. Then, they asked me to sing a song and I said, 'Oh, I didn't know a song was required.'" She continues, "They told me to just sing anything, so I took a deep breath, looked this man in the eye, and with a brassy seductive stare, I started to sing 'You better watch out, you better not cry, you better not pout, I'm telling you why, Santa Claus is coming to town.' I did it in a vampy seductive way and sang the whole three verses. They thanked me and I left."

Jasmine said that this was an especially important day for her, because she now knew that if she was able to go to such "absurd lengths" for an audition, she was able to do anything. "It gave me the courage to do more and affirmed my love of acting. I was now able to say to myself, 'Yes, I am an actress!'"

LU ROSS — *Master Chef, Caucasian, 43*
SHERRY HILASKI — *Midwife, Caucasian, 40*
LAUREL KING — *Writer, Caucasian, 39*

This was going to be our big night out on the town. We had all managed to find child care on the same night. As we drove to the restaurant where we were to celebrate Sherry's fortieth birthday, we all wondered if we should take a nap in the car first. The kids had kept us running and we were feeling a bit ragged.

Lu was driving, and I was sure Sherry would fall asleep before we could get her to dinner. After we sat down and ordered our meals, we livened up a bit. We laughed about finally having this alone time together, yet we could hardly stay awake. "Ah, would Murphy Brown be like this?" I thought.

The conversation turned to what I was writing about. Lu said, "Wild women, hmm," and said to Sherry, "I'm not a wild woman, are you?" Sherry responded with a yawn, "Not at the moment." I hoped that would finish off the conversation and we could move onto the latest films (of course, my favorite topic).

But Lu, who built her own home, opened her own restaurant and had her first child at forty-one, continued to reflect on my book. She spoke of the wild women she knew and felt passionate about people such as Isadora Duncan and Lou Andreas. We spoke of their lives, their bravery, their affect on the world. I noticed Lu, who is usually ready for bed early, was getting more energized.

We left the restaurant and Lu suggested that she show us some of the special gardens she knows of in Mendocino. We followed her and actually became more awake. There was a full moon and we could see the flowers, the brick-laid paths, the old enchanted homes. Then, Lu suggested she drive us around the area a bit. We agreed, but Sherry and I were practically falling asleep on each other's shoulders in the back seat (the child safety seat was in the front seat).

We grew more alert when we thought Lu was going to drive us off a cliff in order to show us this spectacular moonlit view of the ocean. We continued our sightseeing and finally suggested it might be time to head home. Lu had one more place she had to show us. We were driven to a circle of beautiful redwoods and, as we got out of the car and stood staring up at the majestic trees, Sherry and I turned in unison and saw Lu's face silhouetted before the moon. Sherry said, "Now *there's* a wild woman."

7
Protecting
Your Wild Side

Women are frightened of unleashing their wild side because they don't feel safe, but feeling safe is essential if we are to reveal our true selves. As one wise woman said, "We need to overcome our fear of man." It is time to realize how much power we really do have. To do that, we must first acknowledge our denial of how repressed we really are.

For centuries we have been indoctrinated into seeing ourselves as the "weaker" sex, referring to the physical but leading us to buy a larger package. For one thing, how would anyone know who's physically stronger when little girls are constantly stopped from fighting? After all, it's not "ladylike." Overall, in upper-body strength and size, it is true that most men hold more strength; however, challenging new facts proclaim women capable of greater lower-body strength. Many women are in training to change their levels of physical strength. Women are also becoming more attuned to applying the power of their minds, emotions and spirits as means of protection.

No wonder women are frightened of men. For at least three thousand years, men have successfully managed to dominate women. Women are afraid to walk the streets alone, to ride buses and subways and even sleep in their own beds. We have only to watch the news to know that large numbers of women are being battered, raped, mugged, incested and sexually harassed on an hourly basis.

The rape and pillage system is still in play. As we face the truth, we see that our society is set up to protect those in power, not just men, but the patriarchal system. A woman may be battered for years by her partner and then, one day, while pushed to the edge, she strikes back with a weapon and kills him. She is sent to prison for second-degree murder. In addition, she is often given twice as long of a sentence as a man for the same offense. Evidence of a woman being battered year after year, the Battered Woman Syndrome, is admissible as evidence during a trial in only two of our fifty states.

Rape victims are haunted for years by the fear that the rapist will return. Yet, if a weapon is used in self-defense, the victim must prove the person who entered their home was going to attack and/or rape them. More often than not, that proof is revealed through humiliating and abusive questions based on the victim's private life.

Since the system is currently inadequate, many women are literally taking matters into their own hands. A large and growing movement of women's self-defense classes is being integrated into our society. Women are also increasingly aware that protection involves a holistic approach — the emotional, spiritual and mental powers a woman can use to build her self-worth — including the knowledge that she does not deserve to be attacked. Without this kind of thinking, the cycle of abuse continues.

Physical Protection

It is vital for women to listen to the cues they are receiving from their bodies. If we train ourselves to listen then, like the wild animal, we will begin to sense danger. For example, at some time you may have felt the hair stand up on the back of your neck, or suddenly you turned cold all over. If you receive such warning signs from your body, it's time to heighten your awareness, look around, perhaps cross the street to avoid someone, or leave the room if you're sharing it with a potentially violent person.

Know your environment. Lock the office door if you're the only one in the building. If you're walking from the office to your car, be alert and have your keys in your hand instead of fumbling for them in your purse. When you get home, lock your door (double bolts are recommended) and before bedtime, lock any windows that may be accessible from the ground floor. These suggestions may sound overly vigilant, but if you have been attacked or read about assaults in the news, you know that these measures can avoid a traumatic event.

A majority of violence toward women is domestic and, even though hopelessness runs strong among women in this situation, there are solutions. However, it takes that first cry for help — talking to a friend or counselor — to finally realize that a new way of life is possible. The battered woman can leave; there are shelters and what has happened is not their fault.

You may never need to protect yourself physically but, if you do, it can be very empowering for you to know how to defend yourself. Women are increasingly working out in gyms, building strength and stamina. Boxing has taken off in the larger cities and a variety of self-defense classes are being offered.

Some people are afraid that if they learn to defend themselves, they'll physically invite trouble. More lies. This is probably some ancient fear that was instilled in us. However, if you carry this fear, you can always ask of your Higher Power or inner self that you do not draw in any challenges that would be frightening or harmful to you.

A sixteen-year-old girl, Yuma, was regularly being picked on and beat up by a group of girls at her high school. It was terrifying for her to show up at school not knowing when the next attack would be. Her mother took her to a four-day, self-defense class. At the end, she had not only worked out rage from an earlier childhood attack, but she now had the skills to take care of herself. When one of the group of girls approached her and started with the usual verbal jabbing, instead of trying to slink away Yuma looked her straight in the eyes and answered with a strong response. The other girl sensed that Yuma would rise to her challenge and left. Yuma was *never* bothered again.

Self-defense classes teach women to use their voices — getting angry and yelling "No" is highly effective. Py Bateman, director of Alternatives to Fear, states women who are least likely to get raped are those who respond with anger. They are able to fight, claw and scream, "No, get away from me!" Of course, if someone is holding a weapon on you — a knife, for example — depending on your instincts and training, you might move physically against the person. However, if someone is holding a loaded gun on you, it is recommended not to resort to physical action unless you see a clear opening for kicking the gun out of reach.

Many classes are developing into a mixture of martial arts and street-fighting. Women learn to free themselves from neck, head, leg or hand holds, how to move against the attacker and do enough damage to get away.

The Los Angeles Commission on Assaults Against Women teaches that a woman's best defense is herself. They discuss self-esteem, learning to feel that you are worth fighting for. Strength is not necessarily a requirement. They teach street-fighting methods that are especially created for a woman who is smaller than her aggressor. Women learn techniques that target a man's most vulnerable areas including eyes, nose, throat, groin and knees. The combination of hitting one or more of these places while also using your voice is very effective in freeing yourself. Women learn that, as in martial art classes, staying focused is vital. Balance and the power to follow through with the techniques make a big difference. Refuse to see yourself as the victim.

Many women are afraid of doing long-term damage to their attacker, yet how many assailants think about this? Think of the years it takes to recover from an attack; depending on the degree of damage, it can take a lifetime. Then, recovered physically or not, no one ever forgets.

Dawn Callan, of San Anselmo, teaches Awakening the Warrior Within classes. She is a black belt in Kobra Kay and Pen Po karate, martial arts, which stresses street-fighting. She teaches awareness exercises, communication skills and self-defense techniques. She believes ". . . it is the woman's warrior energy that initiates action, takes risks and defines boundaries.

Women learn to disarm and attack, act with one hundred percent commitment. Callan and Associates have taught over three thousand participants; six of them who have subsequently been attacked, have all successfully escaped. Women learn to pull from inner resources, drawing upon a part of themselves that knows how to deal with an attack." In her class, women do not learn to be "nice" and "polite" as they move into an attack. They use the force and power of the warrior.

Most importantly, rape crisis centers stress, "Don't judge yourself." If you have survived an attack, "You did it right."

Generally, women who take self-defense courses are those who are healing from a traumatic event, or who are in touch with the wild woman who wants to know she is safe on all levels. Unfortunately, seldom are these the women who are in the middle of the Battered Woman Syndrome. These battered women do not see a way out. They're afraid to take defense classes for fear of the abuse that could result if they are discovered. The despair is tremendous but there is a way out. As more and more women are taking steps to protect themselves, the more the spirit of this movement will spread. We can spread the word ourselves by telling a friend or neighbor where she can get help: a shelter, a self-defense class or counselling. Offer knowledge and support. If every woman knew how to defend herself, incidents of attacks and battering would drop dramatically.

Emotional Protection

Wild women often stand out because they have chosen unconventional lifestyles. What is natural to a wild woman may or may not receive support from family and friends. For example, Isadora Duncan's mother came home one day and found that Isadora had gathered a group of babies in the neighborhood and was leading them in hand movements. Isadora's mother joined in by accompanying her daughter on the piano. That was the beginning of Isadora's successful career as a dance teacher. Isadora was six at the time.

When your choice of lifestyle does not receive approval from family or even friends, it's important to have that strong sense of self-worth; know who you are, and what you want for yourself. Isadora did not always receive approval from the public for her dancing or her personal life. Some of our greatest wild mentors admit the hurt they felt from critics or close friends, but they knew that living their lives any other way would have destroyed their spirit.

Self-esteem is an effective form of protection. It means we walk with strength, love ourselves enough to take care of our needs, protect our environment and stay alert when necessary. We take a physical stance that means we can move into a challenge, not away from it. But this also means we know how to say "no," and that "no" is delivered in a way that is heard.

Saying "no" and setting limits comes into play in every area of our lives. We need to know who we are, and be able to separate ourselves from opinions others may have of us. As wild women, we may stand out more; our uninhibited, fun nature can be intimidating. Sometimes others don't like seeing people doing the unusual — it frightens them. But, for whatever reason, it's important to know which is your opinion and which is theirs. If you're running down the street with your friends in the rain, laughing and making noise, and some guy you pass says, "Act your age," you can ignore him or you can say, "Keep your opinions to yourself (you old goat)!"

One of my favorites is the wild woman with the teenager. You're going to a movie and your daughter or son requests that you don't hoot or yell in the theater. In that case, you can choose to respect their request, knowing how painfully embarrassing it can be to a teenager, or you can choose to sit in separate places so you can have your fun and your teenager can pretend not to know you.

Knowing how you feel can be particularly important when interacting with someone close to you. Your risk-taking or change in behavior may threaten a partner or long-time friend. They may caution you, want to offer advice. At times, you may be seeking advice and, in that case, their opinions are welcome. At other times, you may be looking for support for your decision and get the opposite. Most children assume their parents' opinions, and many of us are still running around with those beliefs in our heads. When we challenge these beliefs in ourselves, we may at first experience fear or guilt. It's important, as we spread our wild wings, that we go to those who can offer us the emotional support we need. As we grow stronger in ourselves, we will then be more sure of ourselves when questioned by others.

People love to project their opinions onto others who stand out. Think of all the judgements and unwanted advice a president gets — or the projections of love and romance a movie star receives. Then there are those who believe that authors, "spiritual leaders," or the famous or powerful have more answers or power than they do. Either way, if you are receiving any projections, negative or positive, it's important to hold to the truth about yourself and seek honest support wherever you can get it. Refuse to be crushed, or pumped up, by what others know nothing about.

Emotional protection also involves not projecting your views onto others or asking them to change. For example, Rebecca had changed. Since the emergence of her wild woman, she had become more social and interested in political activities. One of her closest friends had felt left out and threatened by these changes and, every time Rebecca saw this woman, they ended up fighting. They had also become entangled (both in work and friendship) in ways that made it difficult to separate. Yet, that separation had become sadly appropriate.

Rebecca, with some encouragement, had been removing herself from this person. Due to work issues, however, they had to talk occasionally. Rebecca kept hoping things would change, but each time she spoke to her friend, she received another insult. Confrontation, which had been her first response to the situation, had only drained the two of them. One day a friend said, "I've been listening to these stories for a year now. I hear that your real pain is that you expect her to change." Rebecca heaved a deep sigh of relief. She could stop expecting her friend to change her behavior, while she continued to remove herself from a painful situation. We can protect our wild hearts with inner clarity. Just as we do not want others to try to change us, we should not try to change others.

Learning to say "no" can also protect you from forms of physical abuse and sexual harassment. Melissa was being sexually harassed by a co-worker. Her co-worker would move close and whisper, "I know you'd love to suck my dick . . ." At first Melissa was shocked. She became afraid of him, but then her anger began to rise. The next time he did his usual, she screamed throughout the office, "Keep your sexual fantasies to yourself, you pervert!" The whole office stopped what they were doing and he moved away red-faced. She was never bothered again. As it turns out, other women in the office came to her who had been suffering the same harassment. As frightening as it was for all of them, they decided to press a formal complaint. Because of the numbers involved, they had a greater chance of receiving a response. He resigned. Often one woman alone is ignored or, if persistent, is transferred.

Professor Anita Hill says, "How can we capture our rage and turn it into positive energy? Through the power of women working together, whether it be in the political arena or in the context of a lawsuit, or in community service. This issue goes well beyond partisan politics. Making the workplace a safer, more productive place for ourselves and our daughters should be the agenda for each of us. It is something we can do for ourselves. It is a tribute, as well, to our mother — and indeed a contribution we can make to the entire population."[1]

We can learn to say "no" and have it be honored, and we can choose friends who will respect how our wild woman wants to express herself. There's no illusion that living our lives the way we choose is not at times painful. It hurts to receive disapproval from others. Yet, as our inner convictions grow, what others think of us preoccupies us less.

Spiritual

Our intuition can guide and protect us. It can save us from simple accidents, misunderstandings or great danger. Your intuition is that gut feeling or inner voice that lets you know when something isn't right, when a stranger needs help or when to move away from that same stranger. We can practice listening to ourselves, following the directions that come from that spiritual force. The more we trust, the better things will become. You'll begin to decipher the voice of your intuition from that of your addict or internal oppressor. When that happens, the trust is established and your entire journey can be a fuller experience, easier and safer.

Women also use prayer and meditation as a means of strengthening that spiritual connection and increasing the ability to hear one's inner knowledge. One can pray for safety and peace in the world, pray for the power to hear and follow your instincts, or pray for anything you want. The Divine, I believe, does not have rules about this. It's our sense of not deserving that keeps us from praying for personal needs or for support from others. If we were guilt-free, we could easily pray for any and all things. What praying does is affirm that there is a force within, and without, that we trust.

Meditation, like prayer, builds a sense of connection with that power. It's that time spent in contact with the Divine Mother — the Great Spirit, the Higher Power. When people meditate, they generally feel calmer and sense an aura of protection around them. Some people are fortunate enough to live a large part of their lives in some form of meditation. To them gardening, dancing and painting are all types of meditation. It is what brings them in contact with that power.

The founders of Alcoholics Anonymous, who have spiritually helped thousands of people, wrote, "Those of us who have come to make regular use of prayer would no more do without it than we would refuse air, food, or sunshine. When we turn away from meditation and prayer, we likewise deprive our minds, our emotions, and our intuitions of vitally needed support."[2]

Visualizations can also be an effective tool. One can imagine a sunbeam of protective light surrounding your body — a force field — allowing only what is best for you to enter. If you are going into a particularly risky situation, you may want to imagine a group of wild female warriors surrounding you, as well as a protective light. Whatever visualization feels natural to you is what will be most effective: angels, a terminator, a

Goddess. A client of mine felt she needed to learn more assertiveness and warranted more respect in the accounting firm where she was working. She imagined a lion pacing her office, giving her the courage to ask for what she needed. She also imagined the lion growling at any unwanted attitudes, and that the lion would see to it that what she asked for got done. Life got easier for her immediately.

Susan McNeil, priest and friend, shared a powerful example of the force of light in a dangerous situation. At the time of this incident, she was working as a priest in a rough neighborhood in St. Louis. As part of her work, she would talk to people on the streets and offer aid when needed. She carried a sense of safety about her and was never bothered. One day, she was spending time with a woman who was very nervous about walking in this part of town. Suddenly, a teenage boy attacked Susan's walking partner and stole her purse. Susan says the strangest thing happened.

"I was enveloped in this force field of light," she says. "Though I tried to reach out to help her, I couldn't move past the field." When the assailant was gone, Susan could move again. She helped her friend up off the ground, and at the same time turned to see the assailant running away. Later, she couldn't imagine why she yelled these words at him: "You've made a big mistake this time, young man." Something must have frightened him terribly because the next day, several young boys came up to Susan on the street and told her that the purse that was taken from her friend could be found in a certain shop. When they went through the purse all the money and papers were still there.

Anne Wilson Schaef, author of *Society As An Addict*, describes a similar experience. She was living in the East Harlem project in New York while she was doing her doctoral internship at Bellevue Hospital. "I had to walk home at night. I really felt that nothing would happen to me although a lot of my friends were scared. I felt I had a protective shield around me. Sometimes, when I did get scared, it was because I felt my shield wasn't working or my guard was down. At Bellevue, I worked my final rotation in the male violent ward, and I was the only psychologist on that ward who didn't get beat up."[3]

Mental

Our mind analyzes how to put into action what our wild woman desires. It is part of our holistic protection; the physical, emotional, spiritual and mental are all connected.

Our mind is very powerful and it is of great importance to have it on our wild side. It can be our enemy or our friend, our internal oppressor or our healthy conscience. We need protection from that internal oppressor who has caused us far too much suffering. It simply repeats the abusive words of the past so that we can continue to dislike ourselves, or stay stuck when we'd prefer change.

Our repressive voice may start complaining about the changes we are making and tell us, "You'll embarrass yourself singing at the local talent show" or "You'll never make it if you leave this abusive relationship." But, our healthy conscience can support our steps toward change. Your mind can say, "Go ahead, sing your heart out. You're great!" or "You can leave that relationship, there is help."

If a woman is recovering from a traumatic situation, the mind can be part of her healing. Abused women often feel guilt for the abuse they endured. The mind can help them realize it is not their fault, and give them hope to escape a rough situation. Our mind can tell us, "It's not your fault. You didn't do anything wrong. There is a way out. I am strong and safe, and will continue to be safe and strong . . ." Also, if one suffers from emotional pain, the mind can restore hope. It can affirm that things will get better. Our mind can track what we've been saying to ourselves, which may be the cause of our depression or anxiety, and reverse these thoughts. We don't have to believe the first thing we tell ourselves, especially if it's negative. We can challenge the outdated voices.

When our mind comes up with spontaneous thoughts and ideas, we can support ourselves. Our mind can help us figure out what, if anything, is to be done at this time. If it's time to take action on an idea, go for it. Our mind can affirm our dreams. For example, "I am a successful businesswoman making four hundred thousand dollars a year" or "I feel peaceful and happy at all times."

The more we affirm the positive truths, the stronger we will grow. Let your mind be your friend and protector.

Summary

What causes a woman to feel safe in expressing what is within is personal and situational. For example, it can depend on where you live. Women in New York City are very conscious as they walk down the street, especially in certain neighborhoods. They keep their packages and purse nearby and do not flash their cash about. In some places, people think there is something wrong with you if you honestly and clearly speak your mind; in other places, they think you're stupid if you don't. There are different rules for different places. This does not mean we have to follow them, but we need to be prepared for the consequences if we choose not to.

What has happened to us in the past, and what kind of personal messages we have learned about the safety of people, will also affect how we see the world and choose to handle ourselves. If you grew up in a safe and supportive environment, you'll carry that sense of safety with you. This does not mean that your instincts will be less acute; if anything, you will have learned to trust yourself more.

Applying the knowledge and common sense we have on all levels can be an unbeatable force toward strengthening a woman's place in the world. Women who use a combination of spiritual guidance, emotional strength, mental support and physical skills are at least prepared for what can occur — whether it's verbal or physical. And with practice, this does not have to be such hard work. Being wild is often just being yourself.

Chapter 7 Footnotes

[1] Hill, Anita. "The Nature of the Beast." New York: *Ms. Magazine,* January/February, 1992, 32.

[2] Alcoholics Anonymous World Services. *Twelve Steps and Twelve Traditions.* New York: AAWS, 1953-1992, 97.

[3] King, Laurel. *Women of Power.* Berkeley, CA: Celestial Arts Publishing, 1989, 101-102.

8

Parenting A Wild Child

Raising a wild child is one of the great challenges of life. A wild child is very much the same as a wild woman, but the child won't have to spend her or his college funds on therapy. A wild child has a sense of self-love; they trust their feelings which gives them integrity and a sense of knowing what is right or wrong for them. Their instincts, unencumbered by self-doubt, will lead them to new territories. A child who has been brought up to trust and express herself will be able to explore life without having an inner critic denying her or his feelings. They will be able to express their creativity in ways that it has taken us years to realize.

Is it possible to raise an uninhibited child and still want to live with them? I don't know. We are their models. Trying for perfection will cause us more stress and guilt, but as wild women and strong parents, we can try to give them this greatest of possible gifts: their freedom.

This chapter primarily addresses the five years before children enter school. These are foundation years for building self-esteem, although self-esteem continues to be affected by positive or negative events throughout life.

A wise therapist once said to me, "Having a child is like having a guilt machine. Parents can constantly worry about whether or not they are doing the right thing. 'Am I feeding her enough?', 'Is it my fault he's sick?', 'Will she feel abandoned for life if I leave town?', 'Did I choose the right preschool?' By the time we're through with ourselves, our stress level has jumped ninety degrees.

"You're not alone in your worrying or mourning the lack of quality time you spend with your children. This is a societal problem. One mother wrote, 'As new parents, my husband and I signed up for everything we thought we owed the next generation: baby-swim, kidnastics, creative movement. But my children's blank faces, followed by tears on the way home, made me question my investment. Why didn't they like it? Too cold, too hard, the other kids pushing ahead of them. I think we simply forget sometimes that there is no substitute for plain old horsing-around . . . that a caterpillar nibbling leaves is every bit as fascinating as a chemistry set.'"[1]

All we need is to feel like failures as parents. It doesn't help us reach the uncensored us and be models for our children; it only leaves us feeling badly about ourselves. So, while reading this chapter, you may want to turn off your guilt machine, take what you find useful and let the rest go.

When the statement, "You are your child's mentor" first hit home, I was horrified. "I'm not ready for such a task," I thought. So I ran to my therapist, as women were running to me, saying, "Fix me, before I have this baby." Basically, what we're saying is, "I'm not good enough the way I am." But we are. We may need some information, but who doesn't?

Finally, after the panic subsides, one surrenders to the knowledge that we are who we are and maybe we won't do this job perfectly. Also, try as we may, we cannot control the results. As a friend of mine said, "I was nurturing and taught my son values I saw as being important for getting through life. What was painful for me was that he had to try a different path before coming back to the values he was raised to believe in."

For a child to be a wild child, they first need to feel safe. This means having one or more people in her or his life they can rely on and trust. This can start from conception. Some people sing to their child while in the mother's womb, read them stories and talk to them. Before my child's birth, all her Fairy Godmothers showed up with magic wants to grant her the gifts of joy, power, health and peace . . . in her life.

The main thing for a child is consistency. When they cry, someone needs to be there for them. In most cultures, the first few years still fall mainly on the mothers' shoulders, starting with breast feeding. Early on, babies do not know the difference between their mothers and themselves. You can help them develop an unconscious sense of security by being there and answering their needs so that later, as their independence grows, they know they are individual beings.

As they grow and discover this new-found freedom, although much of this needs to be encouraged, they also need limits set. It's important that they learn not to run out in the street and that stoves are hot — these kinds of basics. Then they really start testing your patience at two or three years old, such as throwing food, running away when you have ten minutes to dress them or pulling the cat's tail. This is when "no" gets to be definite. There are ways to go about setting limits without abuse.

I once heard Holly Near address child abuse on a PBS show. She said something like, "Would you like someone to come up and hit or scream at you? Think how these little bodies feel about it." It's totally humiliating.

It's primary for boundaries to be set so a child knows who is in charge. They need to know that someone is big enough to take care of them. Child psychologist Richard Gibb, who practices in Fort Bragg, California, believes, "That children are looking for a solid, consistent protector to keep them safe." When they spit their peas out, instead of yelling, calling them names, or telling them they're bad, Dr. Gibb suggests, "Simple, consistent directions, such as 'It's not O.K. to spit your peas out.'" He says if this does not work, a time-out period — perhaps a chair they go to or a place where they can collect themselves — is recommended. Dr. Gibb thinks withdrawal of privileges as a way of setting limits is sometimes helpful. "It gives them a choice and teaches them consequences," he says. This could be something like, "If you keep throwing the peas all over the kitchen, we won't go for a walk or you'll have to go to bed earlier." This gives them a choice, and provides a clear consequence to the pea party.

However, none of us are always going to be so patient. My friend, Rose, went to New York and actually bought herself a designer outfit. For "jeans and sweatshirt Rose," this was unheard of. However, she had a special meeting to attend and wanted to look just right. Just as she had finished preparing the finishing touches to her look, with five minutes left to jump into the car, her little girl came in from finger painting and chose to dry her hands on her mother's new outfit. Rose wanted to strangle her, but instead ran into the back bedroom and screamed her guts out into a pillow.

Then, she went into the bathroom and found how easy it was to remove finger paints. She came out of the bathroom, still furious. The golden-haired girl looked at her and said, "Are you happy?" Instead of playing the 1950s record, "Yes, dear, everything is fine" or clobbering her, she said, "No, I'm angry." She then explained in an angry voice that she wanted her to wash her hands off in the bathroom sink and dry them on a towel, not her clothes. Before leaving, she collected herself and explained she was no longer angry, and that she knew her daughter hadn't understood.

A child needs to know that anger does not signal abuse or abandonment. Anger, sadness, fear and joy are feelings that they're allowed to have, too. If they're sad, they can be held in your lap and told that it's O.K. to be sad. If they're scared, you can comfort them. If we lie to them about how we're feeling ("No, dear, everything is fine"), they'll get mixed messages. Since they need to desperately rely upon you, they'll push their natural instincts down and trust you instead. If you're not telling the truth, this will eventually cause them inner conflict that will be acted out in frustration and distrust of themselves, obsession or addiction.

We do not want to dump our problems on our children. We can say how we feel, let them know it's O.K., that it's not their fault if we're having a rough day. Then, they'll find out that our moods change just as theirs do. They'll see us feel happy, creative, sad and then happy again. They'll grow up knowing this is just part of life. They will also have a solid foundation for self-trust.

Besides the limits and boundaries we create for their safety, the wild child needs her or his place of power, otherwise they feel they have little say in their lives. A lot of times that place of power can be how a child wants to dress or what they want to eat. You can also give them choices. "Would you like to go to the beach or the park?" For example, when my daughter Lily was about three, she insisted on dressing herself. I let her go for it.

I'd see her pick out blue to go with some pastel and wonder how it was all going to look. I could already hear myself at the park explaining that "She's now dressing herself," so I could get myself off the hook. One day she wore flowered tights without feet, a blue and red bathing suit over that, a neon pink turtleneck over the bathing suit, a red-and-black checkered dress over the whole thing, with cowboy boots as the finishing touch. Somehow, it turned out to be quite a fashion statement!

You will discover where to nurture your child's likes and dislikes. If they want to build and you don't, maybe a friend can drop by to aid in this creative drive. If you're not good at cooking, perhaps your partner can share that interest. An artist, who lives in a famous community outside Tucson, always has paints, glitter, clay, mud and an assortment of things her son can play with. He began building works of art at a very young age.

We all knew that Madeline Kelly Merritt would be famous. She was one week old when she was observing her first dance class and one month old when she played an actress's baby. She is seven years old now and writes, directs and produces her own plays. She is a constant source of creativity. With her, it was easy to know what to nurture.

Some children need to be exposed to a variety of things, so they can discover what interests them. Let them have time exploring; there's so much to see. There are animals, cities, nature, books, dance, music and museums, just to mention a few. Give children a chance to choose what they want and the freedom not to have it fit into a mold. Their interests may change from day to day or year to year, depending on their personality. Sometimes, a parent gets caught up in seeing their child meet a goal that the child isn't even concerned with. Part of not putting them in a mold is allowing their wild sides, as well as ours, to constantly explore.

Does exposing your child to lots of things sound overwhelming, particularly to the single mother, or the mother who receives little or no support from a partner or society? It's not necessary to pressure yourself. No one does all these things; they happen naturally or are goals we move toward. When you come home tired, perhaps you can do one thing together that nurtures each other's spirit — rub each other's toes, sing a song, read a story or just sit together. We don't always have to be doing something to build self-esteem in a child. That special time when they can come home and sit beside you means the world to them.

Part of raising a wild child is letting our own wild child surface along with theirs: jumping in puddles, skipping, going down that slide. Just imagine you're Auntie Mame with or without the money. Vision doesn't cost anything. Look at travel books together so the child can travel to distant places in her or his mind. Let them see *your* wild side — speak your truth at home and in public. Abandon your naked body to a pool of water, let them make something of clay while you spin your pottery wheel. Although they will often observe you working (or perhaps worrying about money or other responsibilities), they will also have been given the gift of seeing that adults don't shut down, that they have fun too, and they can have that and more for their lives.

Often in stores or supermarkets, I'll observe parents trying to quiet their children in order to not draw attention to themselves, or because they think they might be bothering someone. Both stem from shame. The supermarket and shopping centers are excellent places for people to make noise. All anyone is doing is buying clothes or groceries. Let them be wild and make noise if it feels good.

Bobby Golson, who is one of the cast in the documentary, *A Whistling Woman Is Up To No Good*, said she was in a Manhattan grocery store when one of her favorite jazz tunes came over the speaker. "I've always wanted to sing, but I can't, so I started to whistle," she said. "Then I became aware that people were looking at me. I could hear my Mama's voice saying, 'Now, remember, women don't whistle in public.' I thought about it a moment, and went right on whistling!" Now *that's* a wild heart!

One day I knew that if I did not get to a museum, my spirit was going to leave me and find a more cooperative body. My husband was working and there was no child care available that day, so one-year-old Lily came along. Loaded down with ten tons of baby items and a stroller, we entered the great halls (and high ceilings) of the de Young Museum in Golden Gate Park. As much as I hate to be noticed, I refused to be a shush mom.

Lily immediately began to squeal with delight at the majestic artwork and, wow, how those squeals travelled. I began to sweat instead of enjoying the art I had come to see. I thought, "I can leave or stay." I decided to stay. Soon, we were both lost in the art. Then, out of the corner of my eye, I saw him coming — this very well-dressed, distinguished-looking man. He introduced himself and asked our names. He said he had come down the halls looking for us because he wanted to see who this enthusiastic art lover was and he hoped we'd be back often. Then he was gone. As my wild woman has become stronger, I notice that I sweat less in such situations and worry less what others think about me. What a sense of freedom!

As our children's guides, we can encourage their interests and let them experience their freedom. Isadora Duncan wrote, "Sometimes she [her mother] lamented, 'Why must all four be artists and not one of my children practical?' But, it was her own beautiful and restless spirit that made us all artists." Duncan continues, "I have to be thankful that when we were young my mother was poor. She could not afford servants or governesses for her children, and it is to this fact that I owe the spontaneity which I had the opportunity to express as a child and never lost. When I could escape from the prison of school, I was free. I would wander along by the sea and follow my own fantasies."[2]

Many women I interviewed for *Women of Power* lived in small towns and were allowed to wander on their own. This may have spared them that critical voice that children pick up so early. They weren't watched constantly and told, "Don't do this," "Let's hurry, it's time to go," that children suffer within modern society. Worse yet, parents co-dependently try to jump in to settle a dispute between children and make it *nice*, instead of giving them some time to work it out. A child can become overloaded with do's and don'ts that, in many cases, can override their intuition.

A child needs room to spread her or his wings. It may not be safe to let them go wandering, but while with them, you can stop when they want, explore what they see, leave them to themselves. Now, I realize this could mean ten important stops in one block. Will our world be so much better if we teach them to hurry and make it five blocks instead of one?

Katherine Hepburn tells a story about how she had climbed to the top of a tree and her mother's friend pointed this out with concern. Hepburn's mother simply said, "Oh, don't tell her it's frightening, then she'll never know."[3] Hepburn grew to take risks, never fearing what others might.

Most people have a well-entrenched internal oppressor. The magic is how not to pass it along. Part of raising the wild child is learning to be good to yourself, showing yourself some compassion. Just being aware of how you think and feel about yourself will help. Children sense what we are feeling.

A child can overhear their parent say, "I don't like my body, I hate my job, why don't we have more money, what happened to the good old days?" They can learn this self-hate, this repression, as well as feel responsible for their parent's pain. Turn off the *guilt machine*. We can only do the best we can. It's a major undertaking continuing to show ourselves love in a society where so much repression and hate is taught.

Be compassionate with yourself. I'm sure there have been few parents who haven't been caught letting their critic or internal oppressor out. We can't protect our children from who we are — which is human. As this book has already revealed, my critic is in no way healed, yet it's lessened over time and my nurturing voice has grown. I want to give the same gift to myself that I give to my child: a love of self, a faith in my own decisions, a willingness to risk new and fun things, a love of the earth, and what we have to learn from it and give back in return.

There are social skills that are important to teach a child. In our society a child will be shamed if not socialized to some degree. If a good teacher is available, they can learn many skills in a positive form in kindergarten or preschool environment. If they're shy, the teacher will find ways to bring them forward; if they're bossy, they'll discover the other kids don't want to be with them as much. Then they can be shown ways to be assertive without alienating others.

One of my friends, Kathy, works in an editing room and says "fuck," "shit" or "I hate this scene" all day. As a result, she talks like that all the time. It doesn't bother me but it can sound funny coming out of a three-year-old mouth. One day in preschool, her daughter was angry about something. When the weekly speech teacher showed up, the daughter took one look at the teacher and said, "I hate you and fuck you." The preschool teacher simply said, in a nonshaming tone, "Jena, some people use those words, but we don't use them here." Jena said O.K. and continued on with the group. Later, Kathy told me that she was working at cleaning up her language at home, not because she thought there was anything wrong with it, but she didn't want to take a chance that her daughter would be shamed.

Dr. David Elkind writes in *Psychology Today*, "Post-modern parents understand that doing 'what comes naturally' may not be good for children. There are ways to say things to children that are less stressful than others. There are ways of disciplining that do not damage the child's self-esteem."[4] A good example of this is how the teacher handled the above situation.

"Mental health problems of children are being seen by professionals as the crumbling and isolation of the nuclear family which has been happening since the industrial revolution. We live in a world of one- or two-parent families (both generally working), adopted children, surrogate mothers, co-parents, lesbian and gay couples parenting, all who need to reach out to one another to build a safer, fuller environment for their children," Dr. Elkind writes.

A well-known belief held by many indigenous cultures is, "It takes a whole tribe to raise a child." Children are given roaming room and a chance to learn from whomever they choose.

We can build our own tribes or extended families that often replace blood relatives. The need to do this may have to do with our mobile society, or the safety one feels leaving their children with a relative. There's a town in Northern California where many men are not working, so they are taking nearly full responsibility for the parenting of the children while their partners work. They meet other men and their children at the playground or beach. They treat their children with great respect. They're all keeping an eye on one child or another. When listening in on their conversations, you can hear them discuss parenting techniques such as, "No, I wouldn't push the bottle issue."

Having an extended family can mean trading time with friends you really trust. For example, my husband and I were fortunate to have a godmother to look after our daughter. She took Lily at least once a week for the first eighteen months. Currently, there are increasing numbers of single people who are approaching their friends and saying, "I'd like to be a part of your child's life and would like to be with your child one day a week." These people are generous, and many are not interested in being full-time parents. This gives them an opportunity to be part-time parents. A gifted and loving child care worker, nanny, or other parents can also be part of the extended family. There is plenty of love to go around.

Dr. Elkind also says, "Rapid social change is a catastrophe for children and youth who require stability and security for healthy growth and development. Fortunately, we are now moving toward a more stable society. The current generation of parents have, however, grown up with the new family sentiments and are not as conflicted as their parents were."[5]

We are not alone in our challenge to raise free-thinking children. The world is in a recession. Women feel financial pressures. They also feel the pressure to be both worker and Mom, yet the 1990s is a time when people are fighting for more balance. They're tired of the "We have five minutes to get dressed, drop our children at day care, and be at the office by 9:00 A.M." Perhaps soon we'll be able to say good-bye to the old standards. Things are already slowing down. So, if you feel guilty or inadequate as a parent, remember you're part of a societal system. People everywhere are looking for ways to live fuller lives and pass that freedom on to their children.

Chapter 8 Footnotes

[1] Sheffield, Anne. "Too Much is Not Enough." Boulder, CO: *Ladies Home Journal*, November 1991, 76.

[2] Duncan, Isadora. *My Life.* New York: Bori and Liveright, 1927.

[3] Hepburn, Katherine. *Me: Stories of My Life.* New York: Knopf, 1992.

[4] Elkind, David. "WAAAH! Why kids have so much to cry about." *Psychology Today*, May/June 1992.

[5] *Ibid.*

9

Bringing Wildness Into Our Relationships

Introducing your wild woman into a relationship can be disruptive. It means you are ready to reveal a wild, uninhibited part of yourself. Your fresh energy will cause people to look at themselves, accepting or rejecting their own wild sides as well as yours. To some, your spirit will be as if light entered the room, filling it with life; for others, the bulb may be too bright and they will need to turn away.

Relationships

It is not playing it safe or accepting the status quo to bring your wild woman into an established relationship. It means change. In some cases, these are welcome changes breeding more life and fun for a partnership. Yet, where security and control are priorities, any kind of disruption can lead to discomfort or even loss.

    Imagine that your partner comes home from work worn out and, as usual, turns on the television. You, however, slinkily enter the room with a sheet covering only half of your body. This could invite a variety of responses — anything from the television goes off and the fun begins to his saying, "I'm tired, hon," as his eyes barely waver from the screen. This response could feel like rejection. Out of frustration, you push it a bit, and start undulating in front of the television. This could be effective or it could result in a fight. Let's face it, some people are frightened of living in the moment.

Early in a love relationship the fun, wild side is easier to maintain. You are in love, your energy is high, life is infused into your system. Your wild woman emerges whether you know it or not. Somehow, you find it easier to stay up half the night and still show up for work. One finds the energy to jump up in a moment's notice and go dancing, hold each other close, and tell each other your deepest secrets.

Then, something begins to change. Often people begin to see what they do not like about one another, instead of who they fell in love with. The glow can wane and the darkness sets in. Some may ask, "Why is it that we seem to be arguing more, appreciating each other less? Why are we sitting around more, instead of having sex? I don't feel safe being who I am, I feel stifled. Must we go over the bills again?" I am not saying that this happens to everyone, but it happens frequently. The *World Almanac* for 1993 states that nationwide the divorce rate was over fifty percent per year in the 1980s, dropping slightly in the 1990s to forty-six and forty-seven percent.

Often people are at first attracted to that untamed energy that they see in each other. Then, when they begin to fear losing it, they want to control it, to change one another. A man may want "his woman to be less flamboyant in public," yet still exuberant at home. What one discovers is that it is hard to control a person in one area and not take the spirit out of them in another. Because of this, people enter a grieving process. Many deny the problem for years or even a lifetime, choosing to live under the same roof, perhaps living in resentment or comfort, but definitely without the juice. This is an individual choice, just as the decision to look at one's wild woman is a choice.

Unfortunately, there is not a simple answer to what has brought on troubles and waning passion for a couple. It is different for everyone. Some people fear loss so much that they seek security and that settled, half-buried feeling. They are able to open up for a time, but then the doors begin to shut as they grope for safety. Others may start to move past the romance/

addictive stage of loving to a place where they were taught to love as others showed them. For some, that means nurturing, intimacy, passion. For others, it can mean fear, silence, addiction, cruelty or something similar to them all. For those who suffered trauma early in life, love — or what is supposed to be love — subconsciously means pain. Who wants that?

Three-year-old Angie had been adopted away from an abusive background. She was now working out who she could trust and learning not to hit or push the other children at day care. One day she was playing with her best friend, Sally, and suddenly pushed her into a puddle of water. Sally was completely soaked. The caregiver took over immediately, and later told both sets of parents that the most frightening thing for Angie is getting close to someone, so she acted out by physically pushing Sally away. As adults, we often find ourselves doing this by fighting or being passive-aggressive to cause one another pain, reliving our past by playing it out over and over again. Without insight and a willingness to change, people can live in these cycles for years.

I knew I was in trouble with my first husband when the sexual fever began to diminish. We used to joke about how I married him for his yellow ski jacket and beautiful blue eyes. Too bad the jacket wore out. Then, with my second marriage, everything seemed to surface; the closer we got, the more we feared losing one another. Being oblivious of what was going on, we would break out in rage. Finally, the neighbors got so tired of our screaming they asked us to get help. With counseling we began to break through the crust of what was causing our rage and grief, and things let up for a while. Then we quit going to counseling and the rage surfaced, and neither one of us felt great hope in seeking further help. The final straw, for me, was when I began having sexual dreams about Jack Nicholson. Yuck! Sorry Jack, but consciously you have never been my kind of guy. But I can tell you those dreams were something!

Some people believe that in cases like Angie's, or mine with my second husband, it is the safety and love itself that brings our shadows to the forefront. That rings true because, individually, if we can love ourselves enough, we will be able to face what has remained hidden from us before, such as our wild woman. So, this too can happen in a relationship. Trusting, we unleash our hidden passion, rage and jealousy. Unfortunately, if the wrath is directed at the person you are with, this only serves to push you further apart. The shadow needs to be seen, not stuffed, yet not at the cost of abusing a partner, child or animal.

The purpose of this chapter is not to offer an answer to these problems. Unleashing the wild will always have a stimulating and healing effect upon a relationship, whether it looks that way or not. We can no longer stifle the consequences of repression in any form.

Bringing It In ·

Each woman needs to decide who her whistling woman is and with whom she wants to test the waters. It is important to feel safe when revealing a part of yourself that you may still feel vulnerable about. If you do not feel safe with your lover, that in itself will cast doubts you will need to explore. But, for now, it is important to take your new findings to safe friends — people you feel will accept you, no matter what. It is also important to ask yourself what you want from your lover. Do you want her or him to accept your change? Would you like them to be more wild themselves? Are you really looking for a way out? You may have already come to a realization that the wild within cannot continue to live with the person chosen earlier in life.

Shirley had been uncovering a deep femininity that had been masked by a more male persona. She had learned this from her father, and from the male-dominated world she worked in. To succeed as an attorney, Shirley felt herself having to push and control. Her femininity offered her an open and spontaneous side that she felt had to be controlled at work. She would come home tense and frustrated, not able to shut off the attitudes of the office. Shirley would make a list of the next day's duties and forget she had a lover who might want to spend some time with her. The distance she felt from herself, and her husband, was becoming an increasing problem.

Shirley decided to risk meeting with her friends, whom she had not made time for recently. They met at a local spa and she talked of the conflict she had been feeling. She was surprised to discover that many of her friends, especially those who worked in high-pressure jobs, were feeling the same way. Although they liked their work, they had begun to wonder where the rest of their lives had gone. They wanted more time for themselves, for their creativity and friends. The women decided their meeting at the spa had rejuvenated them so much that they would make it a weekly event. In fact, Shirley joined a gym, and added a workout and an occasional massage to her schedule before returning home. She practiced retraining her mind, to close the door on her work when she left the office. She was fortunate that her husband welcomed the changes he saw in her. He was not an overworker, and had felt abandoned by her. Now, when she came home, she noticed him and did not talk about her work. They would take walks together, go out for fun, or sit intimately in front of the fire. Shirley was surprised to discover that by opening to her wild woman — which for her was a more relaxed, living-in-the-moment, feminine side — she began to sleep better, and wake up refreshed and alert. This left her with more energy at work and more balance in her life.

For other women, fulfilling their wild woman with another could mean riding double on a motorcycle at eighty miles per hour or more, having sex in the forest (watch out for the poison oak!), floating together naked in the ocean, running around the house with underwear on their heads, gardening, telling stories, being held in one another's arms, hitting baseballs or arm wrestling. Now your wild woman is probably saying "about time" to these ideas. Yet, when it comes to participating with another person, we need to consider their wishes also. Being wild does not necessarily mean being unresponsive to your partner's desires.

One of the best approaches to including your lover and finding out what he or she wants is to let your partner know what you are exploring inside yourself. This will stimulate more interest and encouragement, or possibly disapproval. Or your partner may become interested in exploring this hidden part of herself or himself, and then you can do this together. Possibly your partner is not interested in pursuing this journey but will promote your adventure.

But some people prefer the status quo. Then the question becomes, "What happens if I meet complete resistance?" Your lover is under stress at work and wants to simply stick to the let's-eat-at-home-and-crash routine. They, in fact, find your new energy an intrusion, an invasion of the set pattern you have had together. If this occurs, fighting or trying to change the person will only create greater polarity. Over time, as you continue to blossom, it will become evident how this will affect your relationship. Are you willing to suppress your wild woman in a relationship and find fulfillment elsewhere?

Most likely the aliveness you are feeling will bring about a more positive change in the family system — although it may push people past their comfort zone for a while. In any partnership or family, if one person grows, everyone has to make an adjustment. In more extreme cases, change may not be welcome, or you may feel that living life with someone who does not match your vibrancy is less than desirable. In other words, it may be time to get ride of the "old shoe."

Two women I know recently said they had it with the "blob" at home, and shortly after they got involved with other men. The final cards are not out on the table, but one of the women voiced, "I was always afraid of my shadow. I thought it would be something evil or ugly. I don't know, but I do know that there is all this joy there, too — I grieve for the times I could not express myself, all the times I could not jump up and down and be excited about anything. So now, it is coming in the form of an affair. So what? If this is what it takes for me to finally be set free, then good. I see where this energy is bringing me. It is affecting my whole life. The funny thing is, I don't feel guilty. I feel like I did the right thing when I got married. I went for the stability, and I got it, but I want this too.

"My husband and I have stopped having sex. He puts me down like my father did. One night, he criticized me for my taste in music and my joy in dancing. I was furious and ran out of the house. I want to experience my joy, laughter, spontaneity. My shadow also holds my sexuality. My shadow holds that 'slutty' fun part that wants to flirt and conquer — that wants to get what she wants. I no longer want her shut away!"

Alice and Liz had felt the spark fading in their relationship. They started picking fights with each other over things that previously went unnoticed. Alice and a few friends began to explore their natural wild sides and what was keeping them from expressing this in their lives. They spontaneously started a wild women's group. Alice would come home and tell Liz what she was learning. Alice felt like breaking loose of the old rules in her work and in her life. Liz was happy for her, but said she did not seem to have the energy. It was almost as though the more energy Alice had, the less Liz had. Still, because it was important to Alice, Liz was willing to try a few things together. They had both wanted to join a gym with racquetball courts, so why not now? They joined, and discovered the fun they had, the exercise, the relaxation of the sauna and jacuzzi. Although Liz initially dragged herself to the gym, she noticed her energy level increasing. This experiment brought new life to each woman as well as to the partnership. For them, that was just the beginning.

Action

A wild woman does not want to be a caretaker dragging an "old boot" along with her — especially not a whining and complaining one. So, being wild together must be a joint effort. As I mentioned earlier, if you have continued to communicate what is happening for you, then you will know whether your partner is open or not to the idea of bringing more uninhibited times into your lives.

You can let each other know what is important to you: romance, flowers, touch. You can lie down somewhere looking up at the sky and fantasize about the wild things you would like to do together. After the wild ideas get rolling, you may see yourself meeting each other at a cafe or bar, pretending you have never met before, and then going outside to fuck against a wall. Perhaps you see yourself taking a few days off work and flying to Mexico to make love in a warm ocean or on the sand of a beach, or leaving the children with trusted people and having a fun weekend for just the two of you.

Perhaps, if fantasizing doesn't get the steam rolling, you may need more warm-up time. To get started, you could have a rubber duck battle in the bathtub, wash or dye each other's hair, sit quietly and watch the sunset, read your favorite poetry or children's books to one another, do some gardening, create a piece of furniture together, play pool, go out to hear live music. Maybe one of you wants to do one thing and one of you the other, so do both.

Your partner really wants to go backpacking, yet that has never interested you. A compromise could be two nights of camping and two nights at a luxurious spa. You may discover that camping really is something your wild woman likes to do — especially if it includes roasting marshmallows, telling ghost stories and sharing a sleeping bag. You may see a different side of your partner you have never experienced before — an adventurous quality. That may add a new dimension to your friendship. Exploring nature will cause you to see the world, including your lover, in a fresh way.

Other ideas for stretching the status quo may be to bring a cat, dog or alligator home, or decide to do something *simple* like create a child. If that is not for you, design your home or bedroom differently, allowing both of your creative energies to flow. It is also important to have music you both love on hand, choices that will meet your different moods: cleaning the house, quiet time, sex on the kitchen table?

You can blow bubbles in bed, catching them before they all float away. Plant a tree together. You can expand your horizons, together — join an environmental or political group, spend more time outdoors walking, bicycling or roller skating.

A welcome relief from talking about feelings can be talking about things outside yourselves: politics, art, or attending a lecture together to stimulate new thoughts. Yet, we no longer have to use conversation in an addictive way to avoid our feelings. Now it can be an extension of our new growth, healthy interests, curiosity, creative expression. We can talk about how good we feel in the moment — sad, angry, whatever — but with less emphasis on fixing one another.

At times when you both feel too tired to do anything, you could plan a *repressed* evening. (If you are going to be repressed, at least have a good time at it.) Lie on the couch with a stack of videos, your cold medicine, blankets to bury yourself under, and then take turns complaining about everything: the noisy town you live in, the coke dealers next door who periodically run drugs in the middle of the night. Then whine about how your bones ache, complain of your boring boss. You can trash your friends, deciding that you *know* much better how to live their lives than they do. And, in between all of this, you can constantly be saying, "Woe is me." It is fun to get under the covers and compete with each other for being the most repressed, the most miserable. Then, when you have run out of things to say, you could turn on the news and discuss the state of the world, surely plenty of depressing material to last a while.

This is *so* fun. Sometimes you can even change accents on each other. For example, pretend to be a British couple. One can say, "How was your day, old thing?" and the other can respond, "Simply wretched, old shoe. I'm considering a dive off the Tower of London. Do you think you and the children could get by?" This kind of bantering can go on forever. Norman Cousins, author of an *Anatomy of an Illness*, believes laughter heals. Who says relationships have to be such hard work? — probably our internal oppressor.

The internal oppressor has influenced all aspects of our lives, including our ideas about sex. So, it will take time to uncover what your true desires are. What is deep within us is often what we learned from our parents, our peers and the media. Experimentation is part of discovering what you like and don't like. What each person desires will eventually come from their heart. I have found it never works well to do anything only because I think I should be as wild as so and so. Our whistling woman has her own ideas about things.

Friendships

Your friends' reactions to your wild woman will vary. Again, you may initiate your actions and ideas with those you know will support you. With close friends, you have most likely been talking about some changes you are experiencing. If they are interested, they will be enthusiastic about the topic. Most women I have talked with about unleashing our wild sides have been surprisingly moved by the discussions. Women have called a few days later and said, "You're never going to believe what I did . . ." and then gone on to tell me a story of something they have wanted to try and now have, or they will call up with some outrageous event they forgot to mention earlier.

I am fortunate that I have always had a group of friends that have been inspirational to me. However, when I decided to write this book, a friend said that the topic threatened her. I believe the uninhibited behavior scared her; it was probably our running around the house playing dress-up or dancing until it got too hot to keep our clothes on. Even though this is not her style of wildness, I see this woman as an adventurer. She charters territories within herself, being willing to face her past lives. She has a strong ability to grieve fully, and she works with guides. Although these are things she mostly does alone, they are no less a part of her wild woman.

You will weed out the friends that you don't want to share your more wild side with. For whatever reason, some women will not be interested in your way of releasing the wild inside. In that case, you can choose to share other interests with them or, for now, they may be less of a priority in your life. For example, if you move to a small town and decide that it is time to try your hand at pottery, and a friend comes in from the city talking constantly about work and carrying her mobile phone in her pocket, opposites have met. You may find that your love is still there for her but, for now, you are living in separate worlds. I am fortunate to have attracted people who play like I do, such as attacking the food in a restaurant (as I wrote about earlier), roller skating, dancing wildly, howling at the moon, dreaming together, seeing the highest and the best in one another.

One night I laughed myself silly after I had been watching a PBS mystery with two of my friends. Right when they had practically destroyed our nervous system with suspense, they announced "continued next week." We were so irate, we kept calling the station using a variety of accents and personalities to voice our complaints of this sadistic treatment. Like a little child, I was on the floor trying to hide my laughter from the telephone.

Then, a couple of days later, with the same friends I was staying with, I raced upstairs at 7:00 a.m. to announce that a great social injustice had taken place. "What! What!" they screamed as they were awakened from a deep sleep. I explained that I had fallen asleep the night before reading an inept review of Francis Ford Coppola's *Bram Stoker's Dracula*. The reviewer had the nerve to say that Gary Oldman had no sex appeal. Well, that was it! We were all in an uproar! I wrote a letter to the paper stating how appalled I was by the review and that Gary Oldman could ". . . suck my blood any day." The letter got juicier by the line, so I was surprised that our conservative paper printed my letter and entitled it, "Out For Blood."

Reading these things may be disturbing you. They probably sound foolish or ridiculous. That is because they are. Thanks to the Higher Power, we are not all alike and our wildness is expressed in numerous and colorful ways. However, if you find yourself feeling judgmental of any of these actions, you may want to look deeper to see if there is a part of you that would like to act in some of these ways.

A friend told me something I found disturbing at first. "Women don't want us to be wild, because if we are, they will look pale in comparison." At first I thought, "No, it will only encourage others to become less repressed. Women won't be competitive or shamed like that." *Wrong*. After more reflection, I thought, "Why not admit the shadow of competitiveness or shame?" Am I wanting everything to be "nice" again? If one woman stands out and then another and another, and they stop being so quiet and "nice," that can be threatening to those who would just as soon remain the same. Many women have hidden their feelings of competitiveness, feeling ashamed of showing these feelings toward a sister. Yet, when out in the open, competitiveness is just another feeling. It is suppressing these feelings that is dangerous, for then they can reappear in passive-aggressive or attacking forms. But once women admit to these feelings, it is as if the wind blows them away.

I have heard women say to each other, "I'm jealous of you because you have it all." That statement may sting for a time, but with compassion for one another we can move on. Jealousy won't kill us, it only means someone wants more of the same for themselves. We can help one another obtain that bounty. The same is true for allowing ourselves to laugh and sparkle more. If people feel threatened by others, it means some part is seeking that in themselves.

If a healthy competition is openly admitted and women begin to stand out more because of it, then hurray! We can also encourage one another's naturalness to emerge. If someone wants to quit her financial job, stay home, cook and plant a garden, good; if a woman wants to study opera in Europe, so much the better. Our friends will support our truest desires — maybe not without questions or concerns but, in the end, they will be there for us.

Short Wild Encounters

Some women choose to have short affairs lasting anywhere from one night to a year. For them, intimacy on a long-term basis is not important. They want the initial sparkle and glow. When that is gone, so is the guy.

Our monogamous society makes judgements about this. There are a thousand therapists and writers who will tell you you're defective in some way if you're not seeking long-term intimacy. Who made up the rule that we need to be in a relationship for the long haul anyway? Is there supposed to be a great prize at the end of the cactus climb? What "short-term" women could be doing is bailing out after they've gotten all the intimacy they are going to get. Many times people are most open in the early stages of a relationship.

I was talking to a Jamaican woman, Glenda, who told me she had just broken up with her husband. I offered my condolences. She responded, "Why, I'll just get another, better one." In her culture, many women see things in that light. Women in our culture might say, "I have to stay with my husband because there is no one else," or "I will just attract the same guy if I don't *work* things out." Just more repressive lies. If your partner isn't loving, supportive and willing to go the length with you, as Glenda says, "There's another, better one out there!"

Women who usually choose this path do so because their passion lies in other areas, so they do not have time to *work* on a relationship; or they have no interest in working out their childhood wounds with another person. They find it is just more fun to have short flings, get the passion and romance when they want it, and leave when things get dull.

Wild women have no trouble attracting people. Others are automatically drawn to their life energy, no matter what age. I have a friend who wears old slippers and spotted robes, always has a cigarette hanging out of her mouth, but does she have the energy! I finally had to leave her home because I was getting interrupted so often by her visitors. It was like an ongoing French parlor. No wonder she never bothered to get dressed.

If you are seeking a certain wild encounter and it doesn't seem to be appearing at your door, you can go out and create it. Suppose you are in a restaurant and this gorgeous man has not noticed you or your wild friends. You could peel off your velcro monogrammed underwear (with embroidered phone number) and drop it where he can't miss it — just as women used to drop their handkerchiefs. Then again, you could always invite yourself to dinner with him. Remember, in wild encounters, you have nothing to lose. The Divine will always reward those who take risks.

10 Our Wild Mentors

A mentor, for me, is someone who follows the voice of her wild nature, who takes risks and is wholly herself. In these women's lives, this led them to everything from worldwide fame to local notoriety.

Why fame? Were they dripping with talent? Yes, many of them were, but still an abused Billie Holiday had to walk the streets of Harlem at age fifteen to get her first singing job. Georgia O'Keefe had to make that inner decision to paint what she saw in her mind, not what she kept seeing around her. Gloria Steinem thought if she informed people of how women were being treated, the world would respond rapidly; almost twenty-five years later she is still working diligently for the feminist cause.

Besides talent and brains, is it the result of each of them following their guts, destiny, being in the right place at the right time or a combination of the above? The point is the act of trust, not the result. None of these women knew absolutely where their paths would lead them. Sometimes we just do what is in front of us to do, while other times we follow a single inner drive. Like these women, none of us are *always* listening to our wild sides. But when we do there's a power, a strength that we can see in one another.

Josephine Baker

One of Josephine Baker's most vivid memories was witnessing the burning of homes and the killing of thirty-nine blacks in the East St. Louis riots of 1917. Hiding and running from the white rioters, she remembered thinking that she never wanted a child to hurt as she had.

Baker became one of the world's most flamboyant, out-rageous, talented, wild and courageous women. Duke Ellington raved about "her looks and charismatic showmanship." Ernest Hemingway called her "the most beautiful woman there is, there ever was, or ever will be." Picasso said, "She is the Nefertiti of now."[1]

She was born in St. Louis, Missouri, in 1906 and fled an abusive household for the stage at age thirteen. Working behind stage as a dresser, she developed her skills as a dancer and then a comedienne. By sixteen she had made it to Broadway.

In 1925, she travelled to Paris with a group of black entertainers called "The Revue Negre." At first she was shocked and shamed when asked to dance with only feathers and beads covering her body. Then, she says, she spent time with a famous photographer who saw her as "all women." It caused her to see herself differently. She stepped in front of his full-length Parisian mirror and thought, "There she is. She has been there all along. I'd never seen her before because I was so busy trying to make folks laugh and like me. There she is."[2] It was then that she performed her bare-breasted, feathered African American dance on stage, and later created the famous "banana dance." Baker became the rage of Paris. French fashions suited her perfectly, and she was renowned for promenading in the streets with her pet leopard. She did not realize the freedom she would experience outside of the United States, and France soon became her home. Ah, the liberty of staying at any hotel, using public bathrooms, and being waited on by white waiters. She couldn't believe it!

Baker had already married twice by the time she was eighteen. She was as uninhibited sexually as she was on stage.

When she met Count Peito de Abatino (who gave himself the title), Baker began an eleven-year relationship that is said to have slowed her other sexual activities. Count Abatino originally pursued Baker to be her manager. His ideas and her talent led her to be the richest black woman in the world.

He insisted she work on her acting, singing and dancing. She took ballet lessons from George Ballanchine. She starred in several movies, among them *Zouzou*, co-starring Jean Gabin (1934) and *Princess Tam Tam* (1935). Although always the glamorous and brave woman, she was also said to be temperamental, erratic and domineering. Her relationship with her current husband was becoming increasingly tempestuous and his health was failing.

Baker did not know how sick her husband was when he accompanied her back to the United States for her first American tour. In returning to the States she expected a warm greeting, but nothing had changed. She was still forced to enter through back doors and to use separate bathrooms. Her opening night at the Ziegfield Follies was a disaster. She blamed the man she loved and sent him away. He died shortly after.

Returning to Europe and her loyal fans in 1937, she met a handsome Jewish millionaire and fell deeply in love. They were married and she received French citizenship. She had already converted to Judaism while married to Count Abatino. She had a miscarriage in 1938 and her fourth marriage ended in divorce in 1942.

World War II had already broken out. Because of her ease in crossing borders, the French resistance enlisted her to carry messages to the allies. She was captured by Nazis but escaped, ending up in Marakesh. She was found, near death, in a hospital by a man who would become her long-time friend, Sidney Williams. She was suffering from bronchitis, the effects of harsh treatment by the Germans and the stillbirth of her child. Williams was serving as Red Cross Director for Special Activities for Black American soldiers stationed in England and South Africa. With effort, he convinced her to entertain the troops. Never liking to sing to segregated audiences, she continually sought to bring the black men from the back toward the front.

Williams says, "Her interpretive gifts were so great. She didn't just sing songs, she lived them, put her whole being into each word."[3]

The French awarded her the highest military honors for her bravery in WWII. "Little note is made of the fact that Baker, though highly decorated by the French government, received no recognition from the United States for her contributions during WWII, and she probably entertained more U.S. and allied troops at the front lines during the North African invasions than the much-honored Bob Hope."[4]

In 1947, Baker married famous French band leader, Jo Bouillion. They toured Europe and the U.S. Appalled by the continued segregation in the United States, Josephine refused to play to segregated audiences and forced local police to place temporary bans on their segregation laws. She also insisted that at least one stagehand be black. (Could that be why she was called difficult?) She was the first black woman to entertain integrated audiences across the U.S. Her ceaseless work to put an end to racism caused Harlem to honor her on "Josephine Baker Day," and the NAACP named her the most outstanding woman of the year in 1951.

Still, the Stork Club refused to serve her. She was enraged and attacked famous newspaper columnist and radio broadcaster, Walter Winchell, for not standing up for her. He counterattacked by calling Baker an anti-Semite, Nazi sympathizer and a communist. Not permanently harmed by Winchell's attacks, Baker later returned to march beside Martin Luther King in Washington, where she delivered a passionate speech.

In the 1950s, she returned to her beloved France where she began to create her famous Rainbow Family. She adopted twelve children of all races and religions, wanting them to grow up with compassion for one another.

Her fifth husband tried to warn her of the expense of upkeep for the villa and her continual adoptions, but she wouldn't hear of any limits on her desires. That marriage also dissolved, and she was forced to go back to work and pay the bills. But even as a huge success, she could not cover the high debts of the villa. Finally, she sent the children to friends in Paris. Soon after, due to her debts, her doors were broken down by the police and she was thrown out of her villa into the rain wearing only a robe and slippers, holding a cat.

Princess Grace of Monaco provided the down payment on a new villa at Roquebrune. Josephine was able to see her children when they were home from school; sometimes in her grief, she'd be seen shabbily dressed and walking the streets of Monaco, asking for her children.

In 1973, at age 67, she played to an enthusiastic audience at Carnegie Hall. Two years later, the owners of the Monte Carlo Casino sponsored a show called "Josephine," which opened in Paris on April 8, 1975. Tickets were sold out long in advance. Two days after the successful opening, she had a cerebral hemorrhage while napping and died at age 69. Twenty thousand people attended her funeral. She is the only American woman to receive an official twenty-one-gun salute from the French government.

Maria Braveheart-Jordan

Millions of Native Americans were torn from their sacred lands, slaughtered or made to work under grueling conditions in this country. The children were taken from their parents to "be civilized"; many were abused or died of disease.

Maria Braveheart-Jordan is a Hunkpapa Lakota/Nez Perce/Choctaw, who between schooling has spent as much time as possible on the South Dakota Reservations. She has also lived and worked on the Standing Rock Sioux Reservation as a mental health therapist. In the 1970s, Braveheart-Jordan began to feel she was carrying a grief bigger than herself. "I felt generational loss and trauma, severely. Some personal traumas, but some that were handed down."

As Braveheart-Jordan sought information, she found Ellen Epstein's *Children of the Holocaust* to be the most helpful in identifying what she and others felt: a generational grief. She says Eva Fogelman, a holocaust therapist in New York, was equally helpful. Fogelman believes that healing has to do with a confrontation with the past. For the Indian population, "there was massive cumulative historical trauma. There wasn't time to recover from one loss before another came along," Braveheart-Jordan says. She realized that it would be necessary for her to grieve for the historical trauma, so that it would not continue to be passed down. She also saw the direct connection between substance abuse and the dysfunctional family. It was then that she made a commitment to helping herself and her people.

Seeking answers to what she saw and felt, she chose traditional psychoanalytical training and work in mainstream agencies. She also experienced her own psychotherapy as part of her training. Today, she believes, "I cannot work with other people without working on myself."

As a social worker she was asked to look at the person and their environment. Braveheart-Jordan saw the specific historical traumatic events, such as the Wounded Knee Massacre of the Great Sioux Nation. She saw that the Sioux reservations had the highest rates of alcoholism, alcohol-related deaths, family violence, suicides, homicides, poverty and unemployment in the United States — *plus* the most limited treatment resources. She also saw that there was something mental health training alone could not offer her people.

Seeking further answers, she says, "I'm an adult grand-child of an alcoholic, so I began to attend twelve-step groups. I saw the power of the group and people at least addressing spirituality.

"It took me back to the source of Lakota spirituality — a lot of the answers lie there. Ceremony cannot be explained scientifically," she says. "Traditional ceremonies have a lot of wisdom. They help people heal from grief and pain, be emotional and accept their feelings." She says healing unresolved grief is a gradual process but she has seen changes in the past years. "People have stopped drinking, now they are going to sweats, Sun Dances, all over South Dakota, even the urban areas." It's a return to their faith and power.

Braveheart-Jordan developed and was the principal trainer of "The Return to the Sacred Path: Healing from Historical Unresolved Grief Among the Lakota and Dakota." Last summer she and her co-trainer, Dr. Lemyra DeBruyn, educated forty Indian Human Service Workers and leaders from reservations and communities regarding historical grief and the healing that would be involved.

Braveheart-Jordan spent the summer in South Dakota making preparations for the workshop which interweaves mental health approaches with the spirituality of the Sioux, such as the traditional sweats and a "Wiping of the Tears" ceremony. Other facilitators included her traditional sister Lona Eagle Chasing and brothers, Lester Obago and Virgil Kills Straight.

Even though Braveheart-Jordan is the first to say that healing the Historical Unresolved Grief Syndrome is a long-term process, she has seen people return to tradition with a significant rise in self-respect. There's more hope, more joy, less helplessness, less anger, less sadness.

Maria Elena Durazo

Maria Elena Durazo is a tough union leader. She needs to be. In 1989 she was elected the first Hispanic woman president of the Hotel and Restaurant Employees Local Union 11.

She first took the job with the union in 1983 — a union at extreme odds. When the seventy percent Hispanic members of Union 11 asked for translation or bilingual meetings, they were told to learn English. The *Los Angeles Times* quotes Durazo as saying, "The open animosity between union members bordered on hatred."[1]

Durazo grew up in the back of a truck moving from town to town. She saw her Mexican immigrant parents work long hours for little pay. There seemed no way to get ahead. Durazo vowed then that she would fight for a better way for immigrants.

Influenced by the 1970 Chicano movement, Durazo was encouraged to pursue further education. Besides working her way through the Los Angeles Peoples' College of Law, she raised her son, Mario, and began to volunteer her time working for immigrants who were ignorant about the laws and needed protection.

The International Ladies Garment Workers hired her to organize their sweatshops in 1979. The garment workers labored for notoriously low pay, working long hours for the designer labels. Durazo was later hired as a law clerk for Abe Levy, who represented Union 11, and later helped her get a job with the union.

Local membership in Union 11 had dropped along with wages and benefits in the twenty-three years Andrew Allen was president. By 1987, Durazo had won the respect and faith of the members of Union 11. She had organized a strong slate of members to challenge Allen. However, both sides complained of election irregularities, so Miguel Contreras from the international union was asked to step in. He hired Durazo to help, which resulted in recruiting new members, starting bilingual meetings and instilling a new confidence in the members.

Salaries of maids and waiters increased over the next three years.

Durazo was elected president in the next election by an overwhelming eighty-five percent of the union members. The *Los Angeles Times* wrote, "Durazo never doubted that she would eventually help oust the old guard, but said she did not imagine that the change would come so swiftly or that she would end up at the helm of the Los Angeles 13,000-member Hotel Employees and Restaurant Union, Local 11."[2]

Besides the increase in wages, Durazo and her fifteen-member board is negotiating for the protection of illegal aliens and for member promotions. Health insurance is also on their agenda.

Durazo shocked many of the city's government officials when, during an ugly dispute with some of the larger hotels, her union released a videotape called "City on the Edge." It vividly contrasted the city's beaches and tourism with the poverty and violence of those who work in a low-paid industry. Union 11 also plans to strike less at the corporations, which Durazo has found at times ineffective. They're instead striking out at the owners, who disclaim any responsibility for the problems. The union plans to get them where it hurts. Being "nice" is not Durazo's goal. Fighting for the rights of her union members is.

Although some political leaders, including past Mayor Tom Bradley, did not care for the video, five thousand workers and their families have medical insurance guaranteed for the next six years. In order to obtain health care benefits, the workers sacrificed pay increases, so Los Angeles has a lower wage rate than bigger cities — something the union hopes to change in the future.

Durazo believes the rise in people's self-respect and the ability to meet their needs is primary in fighting gangs, crime and the welfare system. She also sees that immigrants, who she believes to be the future of Los Angeles, need to be fully involved in the city in order to have a chance for a better life.

Anita Hill

Professor Anita Hill shook the country when she revealed that she had been sexually harassed by Supreme Court nominee Clarence Thomas. Hill told the Senate Judiciary Committee that Thomas harassed her when she worked for him at the Department of Education and the Equal Employment Opportunity Commission in the early 1980s.

Before the grueling days of questioning were over, many women would reflect upon their own experiences of sexual harassment. There would be those who relived a previous experience of challenging the abuse, those who knew they would be further victimized if they said anything, and those who thought sexual harassment was just part of the job. During the hearing, the parameters of what constitutes sexual harassment were disclosed, and many were no longer able to deny what was happening in the workplace, on the street and at home.

Repeating explicit sexual language that Thomas allegedly used with Hill was assuredly no easy task for her. Hill, the youngest of thirteen children, was raised a devout Baptist near Morris, Oklahoma. Her entire family, including her father who had never been on a plane, flew to support her at the hearing.

She received tremendous support during this period. She needed it. The black community was split, some believing that a black woman had betrayed a black man. In one of her rare interviews, she told *Essence* magazine, "It was a tough decision, but I have to live with my experiences as a black woman. It doesn't do us any good as black people to hide what we believe is wrong because it may be perceived as betrayal. It's an unfortunate and awful position for black women to be in. It's interesting that people haven't seen the harassment of black women as a betrayal."[1]

She also stated, "I wasn't duped by the Senate. The whole process was trying to paint me as an arch conservative, someone who was duped by somebody else, the scorned woman, someone who was deluded, a fantasizer. All those were attempts to avoid dealing with the issue."[2]

Anita Hill received over forty thousand letters of support, many telling of similar experiences, and over one thousand requests to speak. Except for a *60 Minutes* appearance, she refused most requests.

Feeling a need to leave Washington five years ago, the Yale law school graduate chose to take a position at the University of Oklahoma where she specializes in commercial law. Hill was recently appointed the first holder of the university's new professorship, named after her, focusing on discrimination in the workplace.

Billie Holiday

She is a legend. Singers wish they had her voice, her rhythm, her "Lady Day" style. But would any of them have wanted her life?

Billie Holiday understood suffering. Billie was born on April 7, 1915. Her father, Clarence, was a fifteen-year-old paperboy who took trumpet lessons after school; her mother, Sadie, was a thirteen-year-old maid. They married when Clarence turned eighteen. Clarence Holiday loved Billie and Sadie, but his music came first. He joined a band and went touring.

In Holiday's autobiography, *Lady Sings the Blues*, she says she was loved by her mom who worked two jobs to support them. By the time Holiday turned eight, she was already scrubbing floors for fifteen cents and running errands for a nickel or a dime. It was "yes ma'am" this and "yes ma'am" that. One of her biographers, Alexis De Veaux, as well as Holiday herself, state that she was raped by one of her neighbors, Mr. Dick. By the time the police got there she was crying and bleeding. To add to the assault, the police did not believe that this large-boned, big-breasted child was only ten years old, and accused her of provoking the rapist.

She was put in jail for two days. At the hearing, Mr. Dick got five years and Holiday was sent to a Catholic reformatory for girls, where she was treated cruelly. One day she was punished by being locked up in a room with a dead child. When her mother heard of this, she used all of her resources to have the young Holiday released. *Notable Black Women* states that it was an "attempted" rape. There are conflicting statements about her early life due to her traumatic beginning.

Her mother went north to the "promised land" and left Billie with relatives until she could send for her. Holiday states she was beaten regularly by her cousin Ida. The only thing that comforted Billie was listening to music, and singing day and night. Her idols were Bessie Smith and Louis Armstrong. She said, "I want Bessie's feeling and Louis's style."[1]

When Holiday was sent for, she and her mother found a place in Harlem which was becoming the center of the jazz world. When Sadie became ill and they had no money, Holiday began scouting the streets of Harlem looking for a singing job. She got her first crack at a job in the basement club of Pod's and Jerry's, later known as The Log Cabin. She sang "Trav'lin All Alone." She was an instant hit, and was nicknamed "The Lady" because she refused to pick up tips between her thighs.

Timmie Rosenkrantz and Inez Cavanaugh describe a night at Pod's and Jerry's in 1934 when they first heard what they called "The Jazz Voice of Our Century," the unforgettable voice of Holiday. "Billie lifted a voice that was the embodiment of her strange beauty — the heaven, the hell, the joy, the pain of being a Negro. Out came the music from the depths of her soul as if in constant struggle to reconcile the love in her heart with the hell in her life . . ."[2]

Holiday quickly became the talk of the town. The Apollo Theater offered her a job for fifty dollars a week, and asked her back for other engagements. She spent most of the money she earned on beautiful clothes and jewels, and gave the rest away to hungry musicians.

Lady Day was in great demand at all the clubs. However, remembering her past, she often wondered if she was good enough. Also, in the beginning, some band leaders did not understand her music. Being strong and defiant, she insisted on singing jazz her way. Holiday said, "I don't think I'm a singer. I feel like I'm playing a horn. I try to improvise like Les Young, like Louis Armstrong, or someone else I admire. What comes out is what I feel. I hate straight singing — I have to change a tune to my own way of doing it. That's all I know."[3] As a result, she was responsible for revolutionizing the jazz world.

Music producer and promoter, John Hammond, wrote Holiday's first rave review in *Music Maker*. Joe Glaser, Louis Armstrong's manager, became her manager, and Hammond introduced her to Benny Goodman, who she first recorded with in 1933. This met Holiday's goals. She wanted the whole world to hear her music: "My Man," "I Fell in Love With You,"

"Them There Eyes" and "Mean to Me." In those days, the artists were paid thirty dollars or so for their songs, without royalties. She finally got Columbia Records to give her seventy-five dollars a recording.

She tried road touring, but racism was everywhere. She became worn down from continually fighting just to use a bathroom or sleep in a "whites only" hotel. When the band would try to fight for her rights, violence often ensued, at other times they would just be too tired from travelling to stand up for her. Holiday began to smoke and drink at an alarming rate.

When she returned to New York in 1939, she sang solo at Cafe Society in Greenwich Village. It was designed to be a multiracial nightclub — new for the 1930s. It was there she wrote and sang, "Strange Fruit," based on a poem written by Lewis Allen:

> Southern trees bear a strange fruit, blood on the leaves
> and blood at the root. Black body swing in the Southern
> breeze, strange fruit hanging from the poplar trees . . .

Columbia Records felt it was too controversial to touch, but her friends at Commodore Records recorded it and "Strange Fruit" became another of Holiday's hits. She increasingly began writing and recording more of her own songs. After a fight with her mother, she wrote "God Bless the Child" and soon after that "That's Life I Guess."

She said, "One of the songs I wrote and recorded has my marriage to Jimmy Monroe written all over it. I guess I always knew what I was letting myself in for when he married me. I saw the lipstick. He saw I saw it and he started explaining and explaining. I could stand anything but that. Lying to me was worse than anything he could have done with any bitch. I cut him off, just like that. 'Take a bath, man,' I said. 'Don't explain.'"[4] She said, "My song 'Don't Explain' is the one song I couldn't sing without feeling every minute of it."[5]

Monroe and Holiday were married in 1941. Holiday always drank and smoked to mask the pain of her treatment on the road, but in 1941, after her marriage to Jimmy Monroe, she began using heroin which became a priority. Finally she admitted to herself how sick she had become and she asked her manager for help. He sent her to a sanitarium for the first of many detoxes. Although absolute secrecy was promised, word slipped out. Police found drugs in her place and she was sentenced to ten months in jail.

Shortly after her release from prison, she sang to a full house at Carnegie Hall. But what broke her heart was that she could no longer sing at the clubs which had been her lifeblood as her cabaret card had been pulled.

There were a fair number of musicians using drugs in those days, but Billie Holiday was different. She was a woman — black, famous, glamorous and strong — so the police hounded her constantly, waiting for that next slip. She gradually reached for her drug again, was caught, and spent another term in prison.

Being released from prison she decided to tour Europe, which was uplifting for her. The Europeans saw her as the greatest of jazz singers. Yet, when she came back, she was still not allowed to sing in her beloved Harlem clubs. Her habit progressed and she spent nearly two hundred and fifty thousand dollars between 1943 and 1946. Her mother died in 1944, her father having died seven years earlier. Her best friend, saxophonist Lester Young, died with a bottle near his sax. Between her smoking and drinking, some people believed she was losing her voice.

Holiday became skin and bones and her friends urged her to get help. She collapsed at the age of forty-four and was taken to Metropolitan Hospital in Manhattan. The police found more drugs at her place and came to arrest her for the last time. They removed all the gifts that friends had brought to the hospital, and fingerprinted her as she lay strapped to a metal respiratory machine.

The author of *Don't Explain*, Alexis De Veaux, writes in poetic form:

Jazz.
Her life blood.
Jazz was her lover.
It haunted the many songs she wrote.

Inspired her incredible beauty.
Protected her mysterious gift.
Jazz gave Billie the power of flight.
On July 17, 1959,
her heart began to fail
Then her liver.
Then her kidneys.
Too weak to fight pain anymore
Lady Day's spirit
Went the way of legends.[6]

Holly Hughes

Performance artist Holly Hughes had her National Endowment For the Arts (NEA) grant revoked in 1990. In response, she says, "I think the reason my work was overturned is it is chock full of good old feminist satire, and secondly, I am openly lesbian."[1]

Three other grants were also revoked: openly gay John Fleck and Tim Miller, and feminist Karen Finley. These cancellations were based on the 1989 Congressional decision that equated homoeroticism with obscenity.

Hughes says it beautifully herself in the fall issue of *High Performance*, "The defunding of the four of us wasn't the first problem with the NEA because (a) the NEA is a reflection of the art world that has always been a white-straight-male club that is only now starting to crumble, and (b) the NEA does not have enough funding to fulfill its chartered mission, to represent minority voices, to reflect the cultural diversity of this country. And it's never going to get that kind of money, the kind that's needed to really diversify and decentralize the NEA because that would be the end of the white-straight-christian-male domination of the art world, and that would be the end of life as we know it."[2]

Hughes grew up in a Republican, upper middle-class family in Saginaw, Michigan. She later moved to New York to pursue her art. She started out in sculpture and painting. "Her rejection of the classic artistic strategies is part of a tradition which began in the first flush of feminist artistic theory — the refusal to work in media whose history and significance is male-defined."[3]

Hughes' work is truly alive, erotic, politically satirical and honest. She is not afraid to challenge a system whose blinds need to be removed. She has currently founded the National Fund for Lesbian and Gay Artists.

She has performed plays and monologues since 1983. Her performances include *Well Of Horniness, Lady Dick, Dress Suits to Hire, World Without an End*, and *No Trace of the Blond* on which she collaborated with Ellen Sebastian.

Hughes says, "Even though I'm a femme, a lot of my fantasies are about a guy fucking a woman. I have a dick and I know what to do with it." She goes on to say, "With butch-femme identity polarization, the lesbians sort of fell for a heterosexist view that was the aping of male-female desire, rather than a very specifically lesbian experience. Then came a whole desexualization toward androgyny. Now that's completely changed: women are getting into pussy in a big way, and it's great."[4]

Hughes talks about what an "incredibly fucked up person" her mother was. Not trying to defend her mother, she does ask herself what choices this woman had. Could she have had freedom, or was she trapped by being Michigan-born in 1917 to an upper middle-class family?

"In *World Without End*, Hughes explores her fractured relationship with her sensuous and troubled mother, the tensile connection between sexuality and purity, and her own coming-of-age. Sitting in a wing chair, in a red cocktail dress and pumps, she spins out stream of consciousness memories . . . In an ad hoc sex education session, Holly's mother strips before her aghast, entranced daughter declaring, 'This is your clitoris. Let me show you what she does for a living.'"[5]

Hughes feels that the NEA was originally set up to encourage the new, noncommercial work. Now she feels it is about dead artists trying to play it safe. Holly Hughes did, however, receive a playwriting grant from the NEA last spring.

"Really the prevailing view in this country is that the role of art in this culture is not to *disturb* anyone."[6] If you're Holly Hughes, that is impossible.

Chai Ling

Protesting a corrupt and censoring Chinese government, students staged a peaceful demonstration in Beijing's Tiananmen Square. It was mid-April, 1989, and many Chinese people supported the students' efforts — even thieves handed out pamphlets saying that they would refrain from stealing.

Chai Ling was born in the northeastern province of Shandong. Her parents were communist party members. She was considered a perfect student because she was smart, of high moral character and in good health. In 1987 she began her graduate studies in psychology at Beijing Normal University and, from what she learned, began to question her government. This eventually led her to join the April sit-in at Tiananmen Square.

Twenty-three-year-old Ling was later asked why she was selected commander-in-chief the last weeks of the demonstration. "I don't really know why," she humbly responds. "I did not seek leadership. The group chose me. Maybe because they couldn't agree on anyone else, and I had less ego than the men."[1] It could also be the impassioned speech she gave that became a manifesto for protestors and led many to call Ling "The Passionria of Tiananmen."[1]

Tiananmen Square was a statement of the Chinese peoples' need for more freedom. Many had been terrorized by resident informers who reported on their neighbors. Ling says for forty years the government party made people fear even their own family members. Also, citizens were expected to show ration and identity cards to buy food. "In this environment, Deng Xiaoping did not take to our open demonstration," Ling says. "He used terror to answer us, a peaceful pacifist movement. Now he sits on top of a volcano that will explode one day with terrible force."[2]

Moving through the square, Ling collected weapons from students carrying them. This was to be a peaceful movement. "The non-violence came from my heart, from many peoples' hearts. At the last moment, I spoke to the students reminding them that ours is a peaceful movement. We had the Goddess of

Democracy, the beautiful statue we made. To take up arms would turn it all into tragedy. When I stood in Tiananmen Square in front of many, many people, it was like standing before a great mountain, or a sea. So many heads of black hair. A living stream of people. I felt so humbled. It was a spiritual feeling. It was like music. I'd always felt inferior because I could never really understand music. But I felt music come from my own heart in the square. Whenever I hear music, that feeling comes back. It never faded."[3]

On June 3rd, as the shooting began and the tanks moved forward, the students huddled together singing songs. It was quiet for a short time, but on June 4th the troops moved in with full force and an estimated twenty thousand people were killed. Ling escaped and went into hiding in China. She was aided by the Chinese people, at great risk to their lives. She escaped to France ten months later. In support of her people, she toured the United States in June 1990. She wants people to know what is happening in her country and remind them of the ruthless repression that continues, those who died, and those who are still in prison or in hiding.

Regarding repression of women in China, she says, "But Chinese women are discovering themselves. They don't want to be slaves or tools. In the process, they may lose their traditional position, but gain themselves."[4]

Four years after the massacre Ling still suffers from the memories of that day of death and the terror of escaping. She is currently a visiting scholar at Princeton University.

Georgia O'Keefe

Georgia O'Keefe looked at the walls of her studio. It was 1915, and she was viewing her drawings and watercolors from the last year. She felt ". . . disgusted with it all and am glad I'm disgusted,"[1] realizing that the work she had done was all for someone else. She sat staring, and then life began anew. There were abstract shapes in her mind, unlike any she had been taught. "This thing that is your own is so close to you, often you never realize it's there," she later explained. "I visualize things clearly. I could think of a whole string of things I'd like to put down, but I'd never thought of doing it because I'd never seen anything like it."[2]

She stripped the walls of her last year's work, no longer wanting to be influenced by anyone but herself. At twenty-seven she started over again, using charcoal.

Georgia O'Keefe was born on November 15, 1887, on her family's Wisconsin farm in the small settlement of Sun Prairie. She was the second of seven children. In *Georgia O'Keefe*, she states, "I seem to be one of the few people I knew of to have no complaints against my first twelve years,"[3] although she does say she and her mother never agreed on anything.

Georgia O'Keefe wrote that one of her first memories was "of the brightness of light — light all around."[4] When she was twelve she spontaneously told her friend Lena that she was going to be an artist. Her art lessons began shortly after at a boarding school in Madison, Wisconsin.

She later studied cast-and-figure drawing with John Vanderpool at the Art Institute of Chicago from 1905 to 1906. She then attended the Art Students League in New York from 1907 to 1908. She studied with William Merrit Chase and Francis Luis Mora and she won a still life of a dead rabbit beside a copper pot. Later she would say, "Who wants to paint dead rabbits?"[5]

This was a difficult time for O'Keefe. She gave up on her painting for several years, thinking that this was it, there was nothing more anyone could teach her and she'd done the best that she could. She taught school in Texas and South Carolina.

Finally, her sister talked her into exploring art with Arthur Dow and Alon Bement. In her biography she states, "It was Arthur Dow who affected my start, who helped me to find something of my own. He taught me to fill space with something beautiful."[6] She would later write of Dow to her friend, Anita Pollitizer, that his pictures seemed tame to her.

O'Keefe drew the pictures in her mind. She sent her charcoals to her friend, Pollitizer, who wrote that they were filled with strong emotions. Pollitizer was so moved by one group of drawings that she took them to Arthur Stieglitz's famous "291" Gallery. He agreed to look at the drawings. He was deeply moved and asked Pollitizer to inform O'Keefe of his strong admiration for her work. He would be willing to show them.

Stieglitz hung her show in the spring and it was a great success. He made one mistake: he did not inform O'Keefe of his venture. When she heard what happened, she angrily went to New York and asked him to remove her paintings. He would hear nothing of this, and she eventually conceded. The attraction between them was mutual. She received beautiful letters from him as she continued to teach on the open plains of Texas. In 1918, she moved to New York and they lived together from 1918 to 1924, when he convinced her to marry him. During those first few years of their affair, he took two hundred photographic portraits of O'Keefe — a most beautiful and erotic woman.

At Stieglitz's summer home, where O'Keefe felt overrun by people and the greenness of the area, she began to paint flowers. O'Keefe wanted people to see what she saw in a flower and knew that if she painted them normal size, they would go unnoticed. Hence, the year 1919 began the prolific painting of her larger-than-life flowers.

For many, the paintings were erotic, although O'Keefe always denied that this was her intent. She said these were others' projections. When she showed her first one to Stieglitz, he said, "What do you suppose you're going to do with that?"[7] Although her flowers gave her fresh energy, O'Keefe was beginning to feel a need for a change.

Dorothy Brett, Mable Dodge-Lulan and Tony Lulan of New Mexico arrived in New York in 1928. Brett and O'Keefe became quite close and she was invited to join them in New Mexico.

"When I got to New Mexico, that was mine. I'd never seen anything like it before, but it fit me exactly. It's something in the air that's different, the wind is different, the stars are different."[8] It was home to her. She found a place outside Abique, New Mexico, and later a small place in town. She spent six months a year in New Mexico, and six months a year in New York. She said Stieglitz never liked the idea, but she went anyway.

She would bring home bleached bones she had discovered during her long walks in the desert. She painted skulls and pelvises that glorified the rich colors of the sky, and the power of the mountains seen through them. She says they were filled with life for her, and never had anything to do with death.

Stieglitz died in 1945, and O'Keefe made her permanent home in an adobe that she restored near Abiqui. She also loved traveling, and went around the world in 1959 and to the Far East in 1960.

Later in her life, Juan Hamilton, a potter, became her secretary and companion, and stayed with her for years. Hamilton saw O'Keefe as the most alive person he had ever met.

Georgia died in 1986 at the age of ninety-nine. A few years earlier, she told artist Christine Taylor Patton that her life had been very lucky. "Life is like walking on a knife's edge, I might fall off on either side. So what if you fall off. I'd rather be doing something I really wanted to do."[9]

Gloria Steinem

Gloria Steinem has been fighting for the rights of humanity as long as she can remember.

It started by having two parents she took care of. Leo Steinem wasn't interested in a nine-to-five job; he wanted to make it in show business. Ruth Steinem, a graduate of Oberlin College, was a journalist prior to her marriage. She, unfortunately, had her first nervous breakdown before Gloria was born.

Steinem was born on March 25, 1934, and spent her first fourteen years travelling around the country in a house trailer while her father tried to make a living. When her parents divorced in 1948, Gloria went to live with her mother in Toledo, Ohio. They lived in a basement apartment, where her mother would go in and out of serious depressions and occasionally hear voices in her head.

It was up to Gloria to go to school and take care of her mother full-time. In her senior year of high school her sister, who was ten years older, was able to bring her to Washington, D.C. Her grades suffered due to the trauma at home, but her SAT scores were so high that she was accepted at Smith College.

Following graduation, she went to India on a Chester Bowles Asian fellowship to study at the universities at Delhi and Calcutta. As biographer Carolyn Daffron wrote, "India exposed Steinem to poverty on a scale she had never — not even in her worst days in Toledo — believed existed."[1] Dropping what she considered unnecessary course work, she joined the "Radical Humanist" group which resulted in her writing a guide book, *A Thousand Indias*, for the government of New Delhi.

Steinem moved to New York in 1960 determined to be a journalist. She received acknowledgment for her article in a 1966 edition of *Esquire* on "The Moral Dilemma of Betty Coed." In *Current Biography*, she is quoted as saying, "The real danger of the contraceptive movement may be the acceleration of women's role — change without any corresponding change of men's attitudes toward her role."[2] She then published "I Was A Playboy Bunny" which caused her to be taken less seriously as a journalist, but changed illegal practices in the clubs. In 1985 the movie, *A Bunny's Tale*, was made and Hugh Hefner closed the last of his three clubs in 1986.

In 1968, she was hired by a new publication, *New York* magazine, and was assigned "The City Politic." It was then that she served as treasurer to Angela Davis's committee for legal defense, and became Cesar Chavez's friend during his fight for the poor.

In 1968, Steinem jumped into feminism all the way and has stayed there since. She attended a meeting of the Redstockings where New York's anti-abortion laws were brought to the attention of many. Steinem was a national spokesperson for the movement due to her knowledge and vibrant personality. She soon became well known through media appearances. In July 1971, the National Women's Caucus was founded. She joined with such women as Betty Friedan, Bela Abzug and Congresswoman Shirley Chisholm, to encourage women to run for office.

With fifteen years of journalistic experience behind her, Steinem decided that a mainstream magazine for feminists needed to be started. *Ms. Magazine* would address only woman's issues: work, salary, discrimination, childcare. *Ms.* was given a chance when Katharine Graham of the *Washington Post* contributed enough cash for the first few months. The editor and publisher of *New York Magazine* "agreed to include a shortened sample issue of *Ms.* as an insert to the year-end issue of *New York.*"[3]

When *New York* hit the stands, it sold out. The preview issue of *Ms.* of three hundred thousand that followed was sold out in a week. The magazine had a following of five hundred thousand in the mid-1970s.

Revolution from Within: A Book of Self-Esteem was published in 1992. A decade ago Steinem began to wonder why many intelligent, outstanding women she knew did not feel good about themselves. She also began to wonder about herself and society in general. "During the course of this book, I've not only looked inward, but I've gained a new prism through which to look outward," she writes.[4] Researching many of the world leaders such as Saddam Hussein and Adolf Hitler were horrifying, along with George Bush's overly strict beginnings. "World leaders act out on the international stage the pain and humiliation they experienced as children."[5]

Looking at herself, she recognized the need to reparent herself and trust her own feelings, "unlearning" what that little girl had learned so long ago. She also discovered that what she admits is co-dependence was bred by her upbringing.

When Steinem reflects on *Ms. Magazine* and her life, she says, "I used to feel impatient with her: Why was she wasting time? Why was she with this man? at this appointment? forgetting to say the most important thing? Why wasn't she wiser, more productive, happier? But lately, I've begun to feel a tenderness, a welling of tears in the back of my throat, when I see her. I think: *She's doing the best she can. She's survived — and she's trying so hard.* Sometimes, I wish I could go back and put my arms around her. Since I've felt that wish, I've also noticed that her different images are coming together. The little girl listening to the radio in an empty room sits next to the woman trying to raise money or begging for ads. The very young woman in a sari with kohl on her eyes looks back from a mirror at a woman in jeans and sunglasses fifteen years later. The worried self in a trench coat outside the Plaza listens to an older self speaking at a rally. A tall and round-faced twelve-year-old walks with me through a sunny street, looking in shop windows, enjoying my ice cream cone, and feeling remarkably happy.

"We are so many selves. It's not just the long-ago child within us who needs tenderness and inclusion, but the person we were last year, wanted to be yesterday, tried to become in one job or in one winter, in one love affair or in one house where even now, we can close our eyes and smell the rooms.

"What brings together these ever-shifting selves of infinite reactions and returnings is this: There is always one true inner voice.

"Trust it."[6]

Chapter 10 Footnotes

Josephine Baker

[1] Haney, Lynn. *Naked at the Feast.* New York: Dodd Mead, 1981.

[2] Produced by John Kemeny, Directed by Brian Gibson, starring Lynn Whitfield, "The Josephine Baker Story," Home Box Office, Inc. and Angelia Television LTD, 1991.

[3] Whitaker, Charles. "The Real-Life Josephine Baker: What the Movie Didn't Tell You." *Ebony*, June 1991, 28.

[4] *Ibid.*, 31.

Maria Braveheart-Jordan

[1] Interview.

Maria Elena Durazo

[1] Hernandez, Marita. "Latina Leads Takeover of Union From Anglo Males." *Los Angeles Times*, May 1989.

[2] *Ibid.*

Anita Hill

[1] Nelson, Jill. "Anita Hill, No Regrets." *Essence*, 1992, 54.

[2] *Ibid.*, 116.

Billie Holiday

[1] Stephens, Robert W. and Billie Holiday. "Lady Day." *Notable Black American Women*. Detroit: Gale Research, Inc., 1992, 498.

[2] *Ibid.*, 499.

[3] Gleason, Ralph J. *Celebrating the Duke*. Boston: Little Brown and Company, 1975, 778.

[4] Holiday, Billie with Dufty, William. *Lady Sings the Blues*. New York: Doubleday, 1956, 96.

[5] *Ibid.*, 4, 96.

[6] De Veaux, Alexis. *Don't Explain*. New York: Harper & Row, 1948, 138.

Holly Hughes

[1] Juno, Andrio. "Holly Hughes." San Francisco: Re/Search Publications, 1991, 98.

[2] Licata, Elizabeth. "Let Us Now Praise Infamous Women." Amherst, NY: The Humanist Association, May/June 1991, 16.

[3] *Ibid.*, 17.

[4] *Ibid., fn. 1*, 100.

[5] Hornaday, Ann. "Holly Hughes, Playing the Ironies." *Ms. Magazine*, 1991, Arts.

[6] *Ibid., fn. 1*, 104.

Chai Ling

[1] Morgan, Robin. "Chai Ling Talks with Robin Morgan." *Ms. Magazine*, September/October 1990, 12.

[2] Hoagland, Jim. "A Real Voice From China." *Washington Post*, April 17, 1990.

[3] *Ibid., fn. 1*, 14.

[4] *Ibid. fn. 1*, 15.

Georgia O'Keefe

[1] Lisle, Laurie. *Portrait of an Artist*. Albuquerque: University of New Mexico, 1986, 60.

[2] *Ibid.*, 60.

[3] O'Keefe, Georgia. *Georgia O'Keefe.* New York: Viking, 1976.

[4] *Ibid.*

[5] Produced by WNET/Thirteen for Women in Art. *O'Keefe*, video, 1977.

[6] *Ibid., fn. 3.*

[7] *Ibid., fn 5.*

[8] *Ibid., fn 5.*

[9] Patton, Christine Taylor and Alvaro Cordona-Hine. "Days with Georgia." *Art News*, April 1992.

Gloria Steinem

[1] Daffron, Carolyn. *Gloria Steinem.* New York: Chelsea House Publishers, 1988, 45.

[2] Moritz, Charles, ed., Gloria Steinem. *Current Biography Yearbook.* New York: The H.W. Wilson Company, 1988, 542–546.

[3] *Ibid., fn. 1.*

[4] Steinem, Gloria. *Revolution From Within.* Boston: Little Brown and Company, 1992, 9.

[5] Steinem, Gloria. "Self-Esteem." *Ms. Magazine*, November/December 1991.

[6] Steinem, Gloria. *Revolution From Within*, Boston: Little Brown and Company, 1992, 323.

Afterword

If we can't whistle, then what *can* we do? The wild woman within knows we've been controlled for far too long, and that this control continues. The absurdity of asking Anita Hill, "Who are you to be here? Who is your patron?" The almost disbelief that the ERA never passed.

It's time to reach into our souls, find that wild spirit and follow the guidance of that mighty voice. It takes courage, perhaps a whole change of lifestyle, as you get to know more about your wild woman.

As rapper Molly Jakes writes:

"Ma Ma told me I had a strong heart and soul. It nearly killed her the day she knew it'd been taken. Lying there dying she said, 'Girl, take off that white man's suit and start singin again or your heart's going to stay gone — and you'll never, I mean never, love nothin' again.'"

Have you ever felt that your soul was stolen and you've been living someone else's life? Now, that's *oppression*.

What would it be like to live without oppression? Some of you have already found out, and more of you are on the way. It's almost as if you can hear the whistling voices of the women gathering to make a difference in their individual lives, as well as the lives of those around them.

What would happen if each woman worldwide would say "no" to some form of oppression? I can imagine the earth shaking.

Freedom from repression, whether internal or external, results in spontaneity, fun and the power of our voices speaking the truth of who we are. It also means risk, adventure, the unknown.

I originally imagined this book to be fun and light-hearted, which I hope has come through. Yet, as I spoke with hundreds of women, there was that primal cry for more — a cry that said, "I must live my life."

So much passed before me in the writing of this book. Everything from looking down on my drowning body to learning how to sit quietly with a friend, watching the full moon. I saw that as I opened more to my wild woman, people and nature came to show me even more about her. I'm not saying it was always easy. It was, however, in front of me. It was my choice not to turn back.

So, as you continue your journey, remember: you can say yes or no to externalizing the desires within. Your wild woman is probably not out to run your life, then again she may be. She is a part of you and a worthy voice to be heard. For most of us, the more we listen the stronger she becomes. The wild woman wants freedom for you and you know what *that* means: whistling in the market, speaking your truth, sitting still watching the garden grow and love — that deep love for yourself — the glow of this love spreading into your world.

Selected Bibliography

Alcoholics Anonymous World Services. *The Big Book of Alcoholics Anonymous*. New York: AAWS, 1939.

Bly, Robert. *Iron John: A Book About Men*. New York: Addison Wesley Publishing Company, Inc., 1990.

Brennan, Karen. *Wild Desires*. Amherst, MA: The University of Massachusetts Press, 1991.

De Laszlo, V.S., ed. *The Basic Writings of C.G. Jung*. New York: Random House, 1990.

Dowling, Collette. *The Cinderella Complex*. New York: Simon and Schuster, 1981.

Duncan, Isadora. *My Life*. New York: Bori and Liveright, 1927.

Estes, Clarisa Pinkola. *Women Who Run With The Wolves*. New York: Ballantine Books, 1992.

Faludi, Susan. *Backlash: The Undeclared War Against Women*. New York: Crown Publishing, 1991.

Gimbutas, Marija. *The Goddesses and Gods of Old Europe — 6500–3500 B.C.* Berkeley/Los Angeles: University of California Press, 1982.

Goldberg, Natalie. *Wild Mind*. New York: Bantam Books, 1990.

Hepburn, Katherine. *Me: Stories of My Life*. New York: Knopf, 1992.

Hill, Anita. "The Nature of the Beast." *Ms. Magazine*, January/February 1992, 32.

Kavanaugh, Philip, M.D. *Magnificent Addiction*. Lowerlake, CA: Aslan Publishing, 1992.

King, Laurel. *Women of Power*. Berkeley, CA: Celestial Arts, 1989.

Mead, Margaret. *Man and Female: A Study of the Sexes in a Changing World*. New York: William Morrow and Co., Ltd., 1949.

Orenstein, Gloria Feman. *The Reflowering of the Goddess*. Tarrytown, NY: PPI UK, 1990.

Plato. *The Republic*. Translated by B. Jowett, M.A. New York: The Modern Library, Random House, 1968.

Schaef, Anne Wilson. *Co-Dependence: Misunderstood — Mistreated*. San Francisco: Harper & Row, 1986.

Sjoo, Monica, and Barbara Mor. *The Great Cosmic Mother: Rediscovering the Religion of the Earth*. San Francisco: HarperCollins, 1987.

Stone, Merlin. *When God Was A Woman*. New York: Harcourt Brace Jovanovich, 1978.

Subby, Robert. *Co-Dependency: An Emerging Issue*. Health Communication, 1984.

Von Franz, Marie-Louise. "The Realization of the Shadow in Dreams" *Meeting the Shadow: The Hidden Power of the Darkside of Human Nature*. Los Angeles: Jeremy P. Tarcher, 1990.

WOMEN OF POWER

LAUREL KING

Some of the leading voices of the New Age are extraordinarily charismatic women, and in this vibrant book, Laurel King presents ten of them, talking about their backgrounds, and their visions for the future. Featured are: Terry Cole Whittaker, Sondra Ray, Virginia Satir, Claudia Black, Louise Hay, Lynne Andrews, Anne Wilson Schaef, Barbara Marx Hubbard, Laura Davis, and Elisabeth Kübler-Ross.

$14.95 paper, 224 pages, 6 x 9
ISBN 0-89087-580-4
$19.95 cloth
ISBN 0-89087-579-0

For further information regarding Laurel King's Wild Woman Days, Are You Ready to Be Published? workshops, and private consultations, please call (415) 383-4811 or write to Laurel King, P.O. Box 1081, Mill Valley, CA 94911.